✪ WEAPONS OF WAR
SUBMARINES
1940–PRESENT

✪ WEAPONS OF WAR
SUBMARINES
1940–PRESENT

CHARTWELL
BOOKS, INC.

CHARTWELL BOOKS, INC.
A division of BOOK SALES, INC.
276 Fifth Avenue Suite 206
New York, New York 10001
USA

© 2013 by Amber Books Ltd

Contributing authors: Chris Chant, Steve Crawford, Martin J. Dougherty, Ian Hogg,
Robert Jackson, Chris McNab, Michael Sharpe, Philip Trewhitt

ISBN 978-0-7858-3000-9

Printed in China

PICTURE CREDITS
Photographs:
Action Editora: 20
Art-Tech/MARS: 18/19
Cody Images: 7, 8, 12, 13, 15
Serviço de Documentação da Marinha/Marinha do Brasil: 6, 9
U. S. Department of Defense: 10, 11, 14, 16, 17, 22, 23

Ilustrations: © Art-Tech/Aerospace

CONTENTS

INTRODUCTION   6

Acciaico to Astute   24
BGM-109 Tomahawk to Borei Class   32
Casma to Conqueror   35
Daniel Boone to DTCN L5   41
Enrico Tazzoli to Explorer   54
FFV Tp42 to Foxtrot Class   59
Gal to Grouper   63
Ha 201 class to Harushio   72
I201 to India   78
Kilo class to Los Angeles   82
M4 missile to Mk 48 torpedo   86
Näcken to Oyashio   92
Papa to Poseidon C3   100
Redoutable to Rubis   105
San Francisco to Swiftsure   113
Tang to Typhoon   137
U12 to Upholder   150
V class to Volframio   158
Walrus to Zeeleeuw   165

INDEX   174

Introduction

Submarines

Submarines proved to be a crucial element of naval strategy during World War II.

The end of World War II brought rationalization of the submarine fleets of the victorious Allied powers, with the older and more decrepit boats going for scrapping or target practice. Following their surrender in May and August 1945, all submarine design and construction in Germany and Japan came to a sudden end. But these countries had been the most inventive and original wartime submarine builders, so surviving boats, and future plans, were closely scanned by the Allies. This was particularly true of the German boats, since the merits of the Type XXI and XXIII were already well known. The US, UK and Soviet navies all possessed intact vessels of Type XXI and were startled to find just how much more advanced the German boats were.

These formed the basis of experiment and design in the later 1940s and into the

TENCH CLASS: see page 101

I 400: see page 80

The development of nuclear powered submarines changed the face of naval warfare.

1950s. Attention focused particularly on three aspects: the snorkel, which enabled the submarine to stay underwater; the improvement of submarine speed and their ability to launch missiles against surface or land targets. A pattern was developed of a smooth hull, uncluttered deck, no gun, streamlined fin or sail, and snorkel as a standard fitting.

The geopolitical background of the time was dominated by the hostile rivalry between the Soviet Union and the United States –

each with its allies – forming the Warsaw Pact nations in the former case; and in the latter, the North Atlantic Treaty Organization (NATO), in 1949. The Soviet possession of nuclear technology and atomic weapons from 1949 raised the stakes enormously. A new arms race began, with the submarine an essential element. US production of a nuclear reactor compact enough to fit in a submarine's hull brought about the era of the 'true' submerged vessel that could travel underwater for weeks rather than days or

U2501 (TYPE XXI): see page 154

From the 1950s, the development of the submarine was linked to that of rocket-type weapons.

hours. USS *Nautilus* and the hundreds of US and Soviet nuclear boats that followed, along with smaller British, French and, later, Chinese fleets revolutionized ideas about large-scale warfare.

MISSILE PLATFORMS

From the 1950s, the development of the submarine was linked to that of rocket-type weapons that could be fired from under the surface. As the missiles became larger and heavier, so the boats had to be more capacious in order to maximize their firepower. This led to some strange-

looking designs until massive submarines, which could hold vertically mounted intercontinental ballistic missiles (ICBMs) within the hull, were built. The difficulties and hazards of launching a jet-propelled missile from a submarine included the problems of powering the actual launch, of maintaining stability, and of guiding the missile towards a target. From the early firings of Loon rockets, derived from the German V-1 and launched from a deck-mounted rack on US test-vessels, remarkable progress was made. The United States pressed on with solid-fuel rocket engines,

8

while the Soviets continued for a long time with liquid-fuel missiles.

Nuclear submarines required advanced technology, under strict (if sometimes broken) secrecy. Most navies continued to employ, and to improve, submarines with diesel-electric drive. These were smaller, far less expensive, and fitted a well-tried range of tactical roles and missions. Only the US Navy gave up on developing new conventional designs, though it continued to use existing classes through most of the Cold War period.

NUCLEAR-POWERED SUBMARINES

Although the Americans were the first to make the nuclear-powered submarine breakthrough, with an early class of boat based on the prototype *Nautilus*, what the US Navy really wanted was to merge the new technologies of ballistic missiles, smaller thermonuclear weapons, inertial guidance systems and nuclear weapons into a single weapon system. They succeeded with the deployment, in 1960, of the first Fleet Ballistic-Missile (FBM) submarine, armed with the Polaris A1 missile.

The Soviets were quick to respond, deploying the Hotel-class nuclear ballistic-missile submarine. This was armed initially with three SSN-4 Sark missiles, with a range of only 650km (350 nautical miles), but after 1963 it converted to the SSN-5 Serb, with a range of 1200km (650nm). The ballistic-missile submarine race was on, and it would later be joined by Britain, France and China. By the 1980s, the missile submarine (SSBN) had become capable of carrying up to 16 missiles, each with multiple warheads, that could rain nuclear destruction on targets 4600km (2500nm) from their launch point.

(S-22) OBERON: see page 97

WHISKEY: see page 168

WEAPONS OF WAR

NAUTILUS: see page 94

From the 1950s to the 1980s, NATO and Warsaw Pact submarines played a deadly game in the depths of the world's oceans.

NUCLEAR-ATTACK SUBMARINES

For nearly three decades, NATO and Warsaw Pact submariners played a potentially deadly game of cat and mouse in the depths of the world's oceans – the tools of their trade being nuclear attack and hunter-killer submarines (SSNs), packed with weaponry and sensors. Their targets were the ballistic-missile submarines and naval task forces of the enemy.

The development of nuclear-attack submarines in the United States began at about the same time, but the designs followed different paths. The Americans concentrated on anti-submarine warfare (ASW) and the Russians on a multi-mission role, encompassing both ASW and surface attack with large anti-ship cruise missiles. Later on the Americans also adopted a multi-mission capability with the deployment of submarine-launched weapons like Sub-Harpoon and Tomahawk, designed for anti-ship and land attack.

The main advantages of the nuclear-attack submarine are its ability to remain submerged for virtually unlimited periods, its deep-diving capability, the sophisticated long-range sensor systems that it carries, and the high power output of its reactor that can be converted into very high underwater speeds. The later generations of nuclear-attack submarines are virtually under-water cruisers; the Russian Oscar class, for example, was the underwater equivalent of the Kirov class of battlecruiser. Their combat arena, in the main, lay under the Arctic ice cap, once considered to be a safe haven for the ballistic-missile submarines.

DIESEL-ELECTRIC SUBMARINES

In some naval circles, it was thought that the advent of the nuclear submarine would mean the demise of the old-fashioned diesel-powered boats, a form of propulsion which had carried the submarine through all the stages of its development since World War I. This was not the case.

Only the richest nations can afford the costly nuclear powerplants that are necessary for long-endurance ocean patrol; for other countries, the diesel-electric boat provides a cost-effective solution to the problem of maintaining an undersea presence in territorial waters. Diesel-electric boats also have a considerable advantage in that they are very quiet when running on their electric motors underwater, which makes them very hard to detect. During the 1982 Falklands War, the Royal Navy failed to locate an Argentine Navy Type 209 submarine, the *San Luis*, which made three (luckily abortive) attacks on the British task force.

AFTER THE COLD WAR

While the US and Russian submarine fleets continued their patrols and exercises, the end of the Soviet Union signalled a lower level of rivalry and tension, and the numbers of nuclear submarines carrying long-range missiles were greatly reduced. In submarine deployment, attention switched from oceanic strategy to regional hot spots and theatres of localized action. China, France, the United Kingdom, Russia and

ALBACORE: see page 27

GEORGE WASHINGTON: see page 65

the United States all developed new classes of nuclear submarines, with the emphasis on hunter-killer abilities, and other nations announced their intention to join the nuclear club. Meanwhile, new self-contained power systems and a high level of 'stealth' qualities also brought about renewed interest in the potential of the non-nuclear submarine.

At a steady 25 knots, a typical SSN (fast-attack submarine) will cover 1110km (690 miles) in 24 hours, and 7773km (4830 miles) in seven days. Anywhere on the open seas is within a few days' reach, at most, of a nuclear submarine. By contrast, the diesel-engined British submarine Onyx took almost four weeks to reach the Falklands war zone in 1982.

From 1990, the world political scene has been typified by localized hot spots and problem areas. Although all the nuclear-armed powers kept missile submarines at sea on secret patrol, the number of US and Russian active 'boomers' was greatly reduced. In 1989, over 400 nuclear submarines were operational or under construction. By 2011, three quarters had been decommissioned or dismantled. The majority of remaining boats, and of new builds, were designated SSN, or hunter-killers, though this plays down their versatility in intelligence-gathering, special operations and in firing missiles at static land targets, in the course of regional operations. By 2010, the US Navy had 71 active nuclear submarines, of which 18 carried ballistic or guided missiles and the rest were SSNs (the US SSN force has been cut by almost 40 per cent since 1994; one consequence of reduction has been to extend crew deployment from six to seven months at a time, from March 2007). The Russian Navy had approximately 13 SSN-type nuclear boats and eight missile carriers. The UK had eight SSN and four SSBN, while France had six SSN and four SSBN, and

China was believed to have some 12 nuclear submarines, mostly of SSN type. India is about to join the nuclear submarine club, and Argentina and Brazil have announced the same ambition or intention.

CHINESE SUBMARINES

China maintains development of diesel-electric submarines. The Type 039 (codenamed Song by NATO) was first commissioned in June 1999: an ocean-going SSK with a teardrop-shaped hull. The countermeasures suite comprises just the Type 921-A radar warning receiver and directional finder. The diesel-electric propulsion arrangement comprises four German MTU 16V396 SE diesel engines,

OHIO CLASS: see page 26

four alternators and one electric motor, powering a single shaft. Around 13 Song boats are in service, forming the basis of Beijing's modern conventional fleet, along with the 039A or Yuan class currently under development. Their prime use is likely to be in maintaining Chinese claims to islands like the Spratly group in the South China Sea, and monitoring the US observation-ships stationed just off China's territorial limits.

The next generation of Chinese attack submarines is the Type 093 (NATO codename Shang) replacement for the Han class. Two boats have been launched, and the first, after four years of trials, was commissioned into the PNLA Navy in 2006. The second may also be in service. Powered by a pressurized water reactor and with a new bow sonar and three flank arrays (H/SQG-207) on each side of the hull, it can fire wire-guided torpedoes and launch YJ-82 AshMs anti-ship missiles. It is likely that further Type 093 SSNs (six to eight are projected) will show many detail changes over the first two.

RUSSIA

The cruise missile submarines of Project 949A, built between 1985 and 1996, known to NATO as Oscar II, are updated, quietened and enlarged versions of Oscar I. As standard with Soviet nuclear submarines, they have double hulls, two nuclear reactors and twin propeller shafts.

TYPHOON: see page 149

OSCAR CLASS: see page 98

The Oscar class of Russian nuclear submarines have double hulls, two nuclear reactors and twin propeller shafts.

As attack submarines, these are the largest to be built (only the Typhoon and Ohio class missile boats are bigger) and it is notable that construction went on after the collapse of the Soviet Union, a tribute to their general reliability as well as their versatility in uses ranging from shadowing carrier battle groups to attack on coastal and inland targets. Some of the later Oscar II boats remain on the active list in both the Northern and Pacific fleets, with three currently noted as in overhaul and three others in service.

K-141, *Kursk*, was commissioned on 30 December 1994 and deployed with the Northern Fleet. On 12 October 2000, it sank in the Barents Sea, with the loss of all 118 persons on board. It was raised in October 2001 in a salvage operation carried out by two Dutch companies, Mammoet Worldwide and Smit International, and towed to the naval shipyard in Murmansk. The forward weapons compartment was cut out prior to lifting and sections were later lifted in May 2002. Wreckage remaining on the seabed was blown up. The nuclear reactors and Granit cruise missiles were all recovered. The cause of the disaster was revealed as the explosion of a Type 65 high-test peroxide (HTP) torpedo, triggering another explosion in the weapons compartment,

LOS ANGELES: see page 85

CONQUEROR: see page 40

WEAPONS OF WAR

SEAWOLF CLASS: see page 117

WEAPONS OF WAR

causing the vessel to sink. The blast was caused by a leakage of the highly volatile torpedo propellant, which then came in contact with kerosene and metal. Although it was believed that *Kursk*, in common with other Oscar II boats, had an emergency crew escape capsule, it appears, unfortunately, to have been impossible to activate this rescue device.

Project 955, the Borei class of SSBN, is intended to replace the Delta IV and Typhoon classes. As the fourth generation of Russian nuclear submarine, this class of vessel is well endowed with new features and capabilities. Eight boats are planned in total. The first of the class was launched in 2007, but commissioning into active service has been delayed by various factors. A second boat is completed and two others are under construction, one for possible launch at the time of writing. Further boats will have design differences and have been referred to as Borei-A. None is likely to reach the commissioning stage before 2020, by which time submarine technology could have made further quantum leaps forward in terms of defensive and offensive systems.

UNITED STATES

The Seawolf class, originally envisaged as the follow-on to the Los Angeles attack submarines, was the first completely new US submarine design for 30 years. But only three were built before new strategic requirements ended the programme in favour of developing the Virginia class. Seawolf is nevertheless a very advanced boat with many features that make it a formidable element in the US ocean armoury. Powered by a GE PWR S6W reactor and two turbines, it

HAN: see page 74

The US Navy's Virginia class was designed to take on the attack role in a post-Cold War context.

has a pump-jet propulsor and a secondary propulsion submerged motor.

The eight 660mm (26in) tubes enable silent 'swimout' torpedo launches, but also launch a variety of other missiles and remotely operated vehicles. Combat data system, fire control, countermeasures and sonar equipment, all fully up to date when Seawolf was commissioned in 1997, have been upgraded.

Considerably smaller and less costly than the 'billion-dollar' Seawolf, the Virginia class was designed to assume the attack-submarine role in the post-Cold War context.

OYASHIO: see page 99

Rather than deep-sea encounters, coastal and hot-spot operations were considered most likely. Signals from the masts' sensors are transmitted through fibre optic data lines through signal processors to the control centre. Visual feeds from the masts are displayed on LCD interfaces in the command centre.

It is the first US submarine to employ a built-in Navy SEAL staging area allowing a team of nine men to enter and leave the submarine. With a newly designed anechoic coating, isolated deck structures and new design of propulsor to achieve low acoustic signature, it is claimed that the noise level of the Virginia is as low as that of the Seawolf class. Thirty boats are planned. As of early 2012, eight are in service and a further six are under construction or on order for delivery between 2013 and 2020.

Acciaio

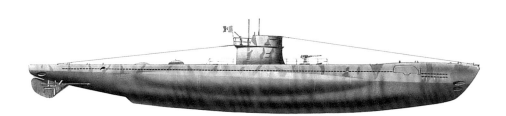

The *Acciaio* was lead vessel of a class of 13 submarines built in 1941–42. Nine were lost during World War II, including *Acciaio* herself, torpedoed and sunk by HMS *Unruly* north of the Messina Straits on 13 July 1943. The longest surviving vessel of the class was *Giada*, which was removed from the naval list in February 1948 under the terms of the Peace Treaty and converted to a hull for recharging batteries. She reappeared on the naval list in March 1951, and was rebuilt and modified to carry four 533mm (21in) torpedo tubes forward; no gun armament was fitted. She was definitively discarded in January 1966. Another boat, *Nichelio*, was transferred to Soviet Russia under the Peace Treaty in February 1949 and was designated *Z14*; she was scrapped about 1960. Some boats of the class were powered by different engines.

SPECIFICATIONS

COUNTRY: Italy
LAUNCH DATE: 20 July 1941
CREW: 46–50
DISPLACEMENT: surfaced 726 tonnes (715 tons); submerged 884 tonnes (870 tons)
DIMENSIONS: 60m x 6.5m x 4.5m (196ft 10in x 21ft 4in x 14ft 9in)
ARMAMENT: six 533mm (21in) torpedo tubes; one 100mm (3.9in) gun
POWERPLANT: two diesels, two electric motors
RANGE: 7042km (3800nm) at 10 knots
PERFORMANCE: surfaced 15 knots; submerged 7.7 knots

Agosta

Designed by the French Directorate of Naval Construction as very quiet but high-performance ocean-going diesel-electric boats (SSKs), the Agosta-class boats are each armed with four bow torpedo tubes, equipped with a rapid reload pneumatic ramming system that can launch weapons with a minimum of noise signature. The tubes were of a completely new design when the Agostas were authorized in the mid-1970s, allowing a submarine to fire its weapons at all speeds and at any depth down to its maximum operational limit, 350m (1148ft). Two of the four boats, *Agosta* and *Beveziers*, were paid off in the early 1990s; the two remaining, *La Praya* and *Ouessant* have been based at Brest since June 1995 and assigned to the Atlantic Attack Submarine Group. *La Praya* was due to be paid off in 1999; *Ouessant* was to remain in service until 2005 as a trials ship.

SPECIFICATIONS

COUNTRY: France
LAUNCH DATE: 19 October 1974
CREW: 54
DISPLACEMENT: surfaced 1514 tonnes (1490 tons); submerged 1768 tonnes (1740 tons)
DIMENSIONS: 67.6m x 6.8m x 5.4m (221ft 9in x 22ft 4 in x 17ft 9in)
ARMAMENT: four 550mm (21.7in) torpedo tubes; 40 mines
POWERPLANT: two diesels, one electric motor
RANGE: 15,750km (8500nm) at 9 knots
PERFORMANCE: surfaced 12.5 knots; submerged 17.5 knots

Alaska (Ohio Class)

The USS *Ohio* is the lead ship of a large class of nuclear-missile submarines (SSBN) intended to form the third arm of America's nuclear triad. *Ohio* was commissioned in November 1981. Boats of the class can remain submerged for up to 70 days. Eighteen Ohio-class boats were in commission in the late 1990s. These were the *Ohio* (SSBN 726), *Michigan* (SSBN 727), *Florida* (SSBN 728), *Georgia* (SSBN 729), *Henry M. Jackson* (SSBN 730), *Alabama* (SSBN 731), *Alaska* (SSBN 732), *Nevada* (SSBN 733), *Tennessee* (SSBN 734), *Pennsylvania* (SSBN 735), *West Virginia* (SSBN 736), *Kentucky* (SSBN 737), *Maryland* (SSBN 738), *Nebraska* (SSBN 739), *Rhode Island* (SSBN 740), *Maine* (SSBN 741), *Wyoming* (SSBN 742) and *Louisiana* (SSBN 743). All USN SSBNs are under the control of USAF Strategic Air Command.

SPECIFICATIONS

COUNTRY: United States
LAUNCH DATE: 07 April 1979
CREW: 155
DISPLACEMENT: surfaced 16,360 tonnes (16,764 tons); submerged 19,050 tonnes (18,750 tons)
DIMENSIONS: 170.7m x 12.8m x 11m (560ft x 42ft x 36ft 5in)
ARMAMENT: 24 Trident C4 missiles, four 533mm (21in) torpedo tubes
POWERPLANT: single shaft, nuclear PWR
RANGE: unlimited
PERFORMANCE: surfaced 24 knots; submerged 28 knots

Albacore

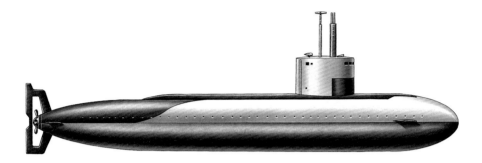

The USS *Albacore* was a high-speed experimental submarine (AGSS), conventionally powered but of radical design, with a new hull form that made her faster and more manoeuvrable than any other conventional submarine. Officially described as a hydrodynamic test vehicle, she was highly streamlined; her hull was whaleshaped, without a flat-topped deck, and her conning tower resembled a fish's dorsal fin. *Albacore* underwent several conversions during her test career. In 1959, she was fitted with an improved sonar system, an enlarged dorsal rudder, and dive brakes on the after sail section; in 1961, she received contra-rotating electrical motors, with two propellers contra-rotating about the same axis; and in 1962, she was equipped with a high capacity long-endurance silver zinc battery.

SPECIFICATIONS

COUNTRY: United States
LAUNCH DATE: 01 August 1953
CREW: 52
DISPLACEMENT: surfaced 1524 tonnes í(1500 tons); submerged 1880 tonnes (1850 tons)
DIMENSIONS: 62.2m x 8.4m x 5.6m (204ft 1in x 8ft 5in x 15ft 7in)
ARMAMENT: none
POWERPLANT: two diesels, one electric motor
RANGE: not released
PERFORMANCE: surfaced 25 knots; submerged 33 knots

Alfa

The second Russian titanium-hulled submarine design, the Project 705 Lira, known in the west as *Alfa*, came to light in December 1971, when the first unit was commissioned. Five more followed in 1972–82. A single reactor and turbine plant drive the boat at a phenomenal 42 knots under water. When British and American submariners first encountered *Alfa* they were astounded, but what was not realized at the time was that there was a serious flaw in the lead-bismuth system of *Alfa*'s 29,828kW (40,000hp) reactor cooling system. The plant was very unreliable, and the cost led to the *Lira/Alfa* being nicknamed the 'Golden Fish'. In addition, the design was not stressed for deep diving, as was assumed in the west, with the result that NATO navies allocated massive R&D funding to the development of deep-running torpedoes.

SPECIFICATIONS

COUNTRY: Russia
LAUNCH DATE: 1970
CREW: 31
DISPLACEMENT: surfaced 2845 tonnes (2800 tons); submerged 3739 tonnes (3680 tons)
DIMENSIONS: 81m x 9.5m x 8m (265ft 9in x 31ft 2in x 26ft 3in)
ARMAMENT: six 533mm (21in) torpedo tubes; conventional or nuclear torpedoes; 36 mines
POWERPLANT: liquid-metal reactor, two steam turbines
RANGE: unlimited
PERFORMANCE: surfaced 20 knots; submerged 42 knots

Aluminaut

Aluminaut became famous when she was used to help recover an H-bomb which had fallen from an American B-52 bomber involved in a mid-air collision with its KC-135 tanker aircraft over Spain in 1966. Built in 1965, *Aluminaut* is capable of exploring to depths of 4475m (14,682ft). She is equipped with a side-scan sonar which builds up a map of the terrain on either side. Most routine underwater exploration never reaches such depths. Even the most advanced military submarines go down no further than 900m (2952ft); any deeper and the costs of hull-strengthening and engine up-rating are prohibtive. For commercial and scientific work in coastal waters, manned submerisbles dominate. Pressures are within comfortable engineering limits, and the crews have made impressive advances in undersea archaeology and oil exploration.

SPECIFICATIONS

COUNTRY: United States
LAUNCH DATE: 1965
CREW: 3
DISPLACEMENT: surfaced not known; submerged 81 tonnes (80 tons)
DIMENSIONS: not known
ARMAMENT: none
POWERPLANT: not known
RANGE: not known
PERFORMANCE: surfaced not known; submerged not known

Arihant

L ead ship of a projected class of six,
INS *Arihant* is India's first nuclear
powered submarine. With the launch of
this vessel, India became one of only
six nations capable of building their
own nuclear-powered submarines. Sea
trials commenced in July 2009 and are
expected to be complete in two years,
with the second and third boats already
under construction. *Arihant* was designed
with Russian assistance, and is largely
based on the Akula class boat. Similarities
between the vessels mean that crew
training will be aboard an Akula-class
boat leased from Russia. *Arihant* is armed
with six 533mm (21in) torpedo tubes,
but her main role is nuclear deterrence.
Her primary armament is twelve K-15
nuclear missiles which can be launched
underwater or through ice. The K-15
missile has a range of 750km (405nm),
though the intention is to replace them
with the K-X missile, increasing the boat's
striking range to 3500km (1890nm).

SPECIFICATIONS

COUNTRY: India
LAUNCH DATE: July 2009
CREW: 96
DISPLACEMENT: not known
DIMENSIONS: 110m x 11m x 9m (361ft x 36ft 1in x 29ft 6in)
ARMAMENT: six 533mm (21in) torpedo tubes; 12 K-15 SLBM
POWERPLANT: pressurised water nuclear reactor (47,000MW)
RANGE: effectively unlimited
PERFORMANCE: surfaced 15 knots; submerged 24 knots

Astute (S119)

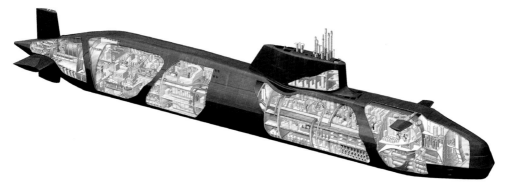

The Astute class was designed to replace the Royal Navy's Swiftsure class of nuclear attack submarines. Three were initially ordered, with plans to order three more. While still able to carry out deep-water anti-surface and anti-submarine warfare, the Astute class is a multimission platform designed with the navy's operational concept of Maritime Contributions to Joint Operations in mind. These boats can covertly gather intelligence and conduct land attack missions whilst operating in shallow littoral waters, which are not traditionally the home environment of the attack submarine. The Astute class departs from the previous Royal Navy practice of building the smallest possible boat without regard to cost, and includes space for upgrades or modifications. For the first time aboard a Royal Navy submarine, every crewmember has a bunk rather than sharing one under a 'hot bunking' system.

SPECIFICATIONS

COUNTRY: United Kingdom
LAUNCH DATE: 8 June 2007
CREW: 110
DISPLACEMENT: submerged: 7800 tonnes (7677 tons)
DIMENSIONS: 97m x 10.4m x 10m (318ft x 34ft x 32ft 9in)
ARMAMENT: six 533mm (21in) tubes capable of launching Tomahawk and Harpoon missiles plus Spearfish torpedoes. Total of 36 weapons carried
POWERPLANT: Rolls Royce PWR2 pressurized water nuclear reactor; backup diesel-electric system
RANGE: effectively unlimited; around 90 days provisions endurance
PERFORMANCE: surfaced not known; submerged 29 knots

BGM-109 Tomahawk missile

Begun in January 1974 as the US Navy's SLCM (Sea-Launched Cruise Missile) Tomahawk developed into one of the most versatile missiles in history. The multi-role Tomahawk missile is deployed in three separate naval versions: Tactical Land Attack Missile-Nuclear (TLAM-N), BGM-109B Anti-ship Tomahawk (TASM), and BGM-109C Conventional Land Attack Tomahawk (TLAM-C). Tomahawk can be launched in encapsulated form from standard USN or RN torpedo tubes, and was initially deployed on Los Angeles-class submarines in this manner. From SSN-719 Providence onwards, it is carried in vertical launch tubes. The first vessel to be declared operational with this installation was USS *Pittsburgh*, which entered service in November 1985. Submarine-launched Tomahawks can be fitted with combined effects bomblets for land attack missions.

SPECIFICATIONS

COUNTRY: United States
LAUNCH DATE: n/a
CREW: n/a
DISPLACEMENT: n/a
DIMENSIONS: diameter 533mm (21in); length 6.4m (20ft 10in)
ARMAMENT: n/a
POWERPLANT: n/a
RANGE: 2500km (1347nm)
PERFORMANCE: 0.7M

Barracuda class

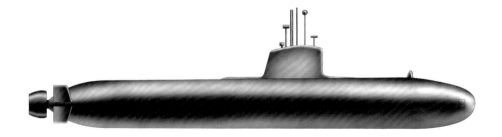

The Barracuda class is a nuclear-powered attack submarine intended to replace the Amethyste- and Rubis-class boats in French service. Although significantly larger than the Amethyste class, the *Barracuda* has a smaller crew and much lower operating costs. It is also more stealthy and can run 'silent' at higher speeds than preceding classes. The *Barracuda* can carry out the traditional deep-water anti-ship and anti-submarine roles, but can also support special forces operations, carry out land attack missions, covertly gather intelligence and operate unmanned underwater vehicles. Armament consists of four 533mm (21in) tubes which can launch Black Shark heavyweight torpedoes and a submarine version of the proven Exocet missile with a range of about 50km (27nm). For land attack missions, a navalized version of the air-launched SCALP EG/Storm Shadow missile will be available in 2012.

SPECIFICATIONS

COUNTRY: France
LAUNCH DATE: expected 2013
CREW: 60
DISPLACEMENT: surfaced 4100 tonnes (4035 tons); submerged 5300 tonnes (5216 tons)
DIMENSIONS: 85m x 8.8m x 7.3m (279ft x 28.9ft x 24ft)
ARMAMENT: four 533mm (21in) torpedo tubes; total of 18 missiles and torpedoes
POWERPLANT: pressurized water nuclear reactor
RANGE: effectively unlimited; operational endurance probably about 50 days
PERFORMANCE: surfaced 14 knots; submerged 25 knots

Borei Class

The Borei class, also known as Project 955, is the first submarine to be developed in post-Soviet Russia. *Yuri Dolgorukiy* is the lead ship of the class, which may grow to 12 or more boats (later vessels will probably be designated *Project 955A*). The Borei class is nuclear powered, and is the first Russian submarine class to use pump-jet propulsion. The boats are to serve in the strategic deterrent role, replacing the Delta and Typhoon classes. They are armed with 533mm (21in) torpedoes, but their primary armament is the Bulava Submarine Launched Ballistic Missile. Early boats are armed with 16 missiles, with the Project 955A vessels expected to carry 20. Each missile can deliver 6–10 warheads, each of 100–150kT yield. The first vessels were due to enter service in 2001, but problems with the missiles caused delays.

SPECIFICATIONS

COUNTRY: Russia
LAUNCH DATE: April 2007
CREW: 130
DISPLACEMENT: surfaced 14,720 tonnes (14,488 tons); submerged 24,000 tonnes (23,621 tons)
DIMENSIONS: 170.5m x 13.5m x 10m (559ft 5in x 44ft 4in x 32ft 10in)
ARMAMENT: six 533mm (21in) tubes capable of launching torpedoes or missiles; 16 Bulava SLBM
POWERPLANT: one OK-650B nuclear reactor
RANGE: effectively unlimited
PERFORMANCE: surfaced not known; submerged 29 knots

Casma (Type 209)

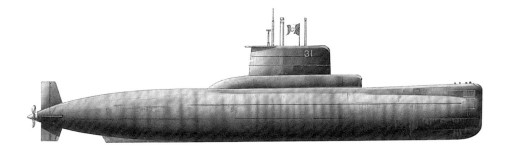

In the mid-1960s, the West German firm IKL designed a new class of submarine for the export market; this became the Type 209 class in 1967. The Peruvian Navy has six Type 209s, named *Casma*, *Antofagasta*, *Pisagua*, *Chipana*, *Islay* and *Arica*. The first pair were ordered in 1969, with two more following in August 1976 and two further boats in March 1977. The Type 209 is a singlehull design with two ballast tanks, plus forward and after trim tanks. The boats are fitted with snorkel gear and with remote machinery control. The type has an endurance of 50 days. Four are in service at any one time, with two in refit or reserve. The Type 209 has a diving depth of 250m (820ft). The Type 209 was just one of a range of coastal coastal boats that were offered for export by West Germany.

SPECIFICATIONS

COUNTRY: Peru
LAUNCH DATE: 31 August 1979
CREW: 31–35
DISPLACEMENT: surfaced 1122 tonnes (1105 tons); submerged 1249 tonnes (1230 tons)
DIMENSIONS: 56m x 16.2 x 5.5m (183ft 9in x 20ft 4in x 18ft)
ARMAMENT: eight 533mm (21in) torpedo tubes
POWERPLANT: four diesels, one electric motor
RANGE: 4447km (2400nm) at 8 knots
PERFORMANCE: surfaced 10 knots; submerged 22 knots

C

CB12

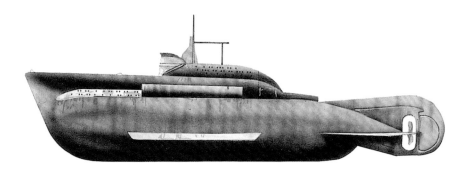

The CB programme of miniature submarines was begun in 1941 and was intended to comprise 72 vessels, but only 22 were ever laid down. They could be transported by railway and were designed for local defence. All 22 units that entered service were built by Caproni Taliedo of Milan and designed by Major Engineer Spinelli. Maximum diving depth was 55m (180ft 5in). After September 1943, *CB1* to *CB6* were transferred to Romania and subsequently scuttled (except *CB5*, which was torpedoed in Yalta harbour by a Russian aircraft). *CB8* to *CB12* were scrapped at Taranto in 1948, and the remainder were captured by the Germans while still under completion and turned over to their puppet Fascist Government in northern Italy, several being destroyed in air raids. Boats that were destroyed in this way included *CB13*, *CB14*, *CB15* and *CB17*.

SPECIFICATIONS

COUNTRY: Italy
LAUNCH DATE: August 1943
CREW: 4
DISPLACEMENT: surfaced 25 tonnes (24.9 tons); submerged 36 tonnes (35.9 tons)
DIMENSIONS: 15m x 3m x 2m (49ft 3in x 9ft 10in x 6ft 9in)
ARMAMENT: two 450mm (17.7in) torpedoes in external canisters
POWERPLANT: single screw diesel, one electric motor
RANGE: 2660km (1434nm) at 5 knots
PERFORMANCE: surfaced 7.5 knots; submerged 6.6 knots

Charlie I class

The Charlie I class were the first Soviet nuclear-powered guided-missile submarines capable of launching surface-to-surface cruise missiles without having to surface first. They are similar in some respects to the Victor class, although there are visible differences that include a bulge at the bow, the almost vertical drop of the forward end of the fin, and a slightly lower after casing. The Charlie Is were all built at Gorky between 1967 and 1972; ten were still in commission in the late 1990s, all based in the Pacific. One was leased to India in January 1988, and another sank off Petropavlovsk in June 1983; this vessel was later salvaged. The Charlie I carries the SS-N-15 nuclear-tipped anti-submarine missile, which has a range of 37km (20nm) and also the SS-N-7 submerged-launch anti-ship missile for pop-up surprise attacks.

SPECIFICATIONS

COUNTRY: Russia
LAUNCH DATE: 1967
CREW: 100
DISPLACEMENT: surfaced 4064 tonnes (4000 tons); submerged 4877 tonnes (4800 tons)
DIMENSIONS: 94m x 10m x 7.6m (308ft 5in x 32ft 9in x 25ft)
ARMAMENT: eight SS-N-7 cruise missiles, six 533mm (21in) torpedo tubes
POWERPLANT: nuclear, one pressurized water reactor, one steam turbine
RANGE: unlimited
PERFORMANCE: surfaced 20 knots; submerged 27 knots

Charlie II class

The Charlie II class, built between 1972 and 1980 at Gorki, was an improved Charlie I with a 9m (29ft 6in) insertion in the hull forward of the fin to house the electronics and launch systems necessary for targeting and firing the SS-N-15 and SS-N-16 weapons. In both Charlie classes, once the missiles have been expended the submarine has to return to base to be reloaded. The six Charlie II boats are also armed with the SSN-9 Siren anti-ship missile, which cruises at 0.9 Mach and has a range of 110km (60nm) and can be fitted with either a nuclear (250kT) or conventional warhead. The Charlie II class vessels are all based with the Northern Fleet, and make occasional deployments to the Mediterranean. One boat of this class sank off the Kamchatka peninsula in June 1983; it was raised in August, but did not re-enter service.

SPECIFICATIONS

COUNTRY: Russia
LAUNCH DATE: 1973
CREW: 110
DISPLACEMENT: surfaced 4572 tonnes (4500 tons); submerged 5588 tonnes (5500 tons)
DIMENSIONS: 102.9m 10m x 7.8m (337ft 7in x 32ft 10in x 25ft 7in)
ARMAMENT: six 533mm (21in) and two 650mm (25.6in) torpedo tubes; eight cruise missiles
POWERPLANT: nuclear, one pressurized water reactor
RANGE: unlimited
PERFORMANCE: surfaced 20 knots; submerged 26 knots

Collins

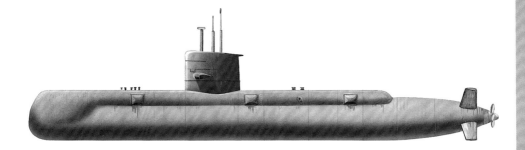

The contract for the licence production of six Swedish-designed Kockums Type 471 SSKs by the Australian Submarine Corporation, Adelaide, was signed on 3 June 1987. Fabrication work began in June 1989, the bow and midships sections of the first submarines being built in Sweden. Diving depth of the boats is 300m (984ft), and anechoic tiles are fitted to all but *Collins*, which is to be retrofitted. The submarines are named *Collins*, *Farncomb*, *Waller*, *Dechaineux*, *Sheean* and *Rankin*; the last two are due to commission in 2000 and 2001 respectively. The boats can carry 44 mines in lieu of torpedoes if required. The Collins class submarines are very quiet, and their long range makes them very suited to operations in the southern Pacific. All are to be based at Fleet Base West, with east coast deployments.

SPECIFICATIONS

COUNTRY: Australia
LAUNCH DATE: 28 August 1993
CREW: 42
DISPLACEMENT: surfaced 3100 tonnes (3051 tons); submerged 3407 tonnes (3353 tons)
DIMENSIONS: 78m x 7.8m x 7m (255ft 10in x 25ft 7in x 23ft)
ARMAMENT: six 533mm (21in) torpedo tubes; sub harpoon SSM
POWERPLANT: single shaft, diesel/electric motors
RANGE: 18,496km (9982nm) at 10 knots
PERFORMANCE: surfaced 10 knots; submerged 20 knots

C

Conqueror

O ne of three Churchill-class nuclear-powered attack submarines (SSNs), HMS *Conqueror* was the boat that sank the Argentinian cruiser *General Belgrano* on 2 May 1982, at the start of the Falklands War. The Churchills were modified Valiant-class SSNs and were somewhat quieter in service, having benefited from the experience gained in operating the earlier boats. When the Churchills were first built, their main armament was the Mk 8 anti-ship torpedo of World War II vintage, and it was a salvo of these that sank the *Belgrano*. The armament was later updated to include the Mk 24 Tigerfish wire-guided dual-role (anti-ship and anti-submarine) torpedo, the Sub-Harpoon SSM and a new generation of 'smart' mines. The Churchills and their predecessors, *Valiant* and *Warspite*, were paid off in the late 1980s, following the full deployment of the Trafalgar-class SSNs.

SPECIFICATIONS

COUNTRY: United Kingdom
LAUNCH DATE: 28 August 1969
CREW: 116
DISPLACEMENT: surfaced 4470 tonnes (4400 tons); submerged 4979 tonnes (4900 tons)
DIMENSIONS: 86.9m x 10.1m x 8.2m (285ft 4in x 33ft 3in x 27ft)
ARMAMENT: six 533mm (21in) torpedo tubes
POWERPLANT: nuclear, one pressurized water reactor
RANGE: unlimited
PERFORMANCE: surfaced 20 knots; submerged 29 knots

Daniel Boone

Although actually two classes, the 12 Benjamin Franklin-class and the 19 Lafayette-class of nuclear-powered ballistic-missile submarines (SSBN) were very similar in appearance, the main difference being that the former were built with quieter machinery outfits. The *Daniel Boone* (SSBN629) was one of the Lafayette class. As built, the first eight Lafayettes carried the 16 Polaris A2 submarine-launched ballistic missiles (SLBMs), each with a single 800kT yield warhead, but the rest were armed with the Polaris A3, which was fitted with three independently targeted warheads; this was in turn replaced by the Poseidon C3. Between September 1978 and December 1982, 12 units were converted to carry the Trident I C4 SLBM. The boats were progressively deactivated as the Trident-armed Ohio-class SSBNs entered service.

SPECIFICATIONS

COUNTRY: United States
LAUNCH DATE: 22 June 1963
CREW: 140
DISPLACEMENT: surfaced 7366 tonnes (7250 tons); submerged 8382 tonnes (8250 tons)
DIMENSIONS: 130m x 10m x 10m (42ft 6in x 32ft 10in x 32ft 10in)
ARMAMENT: sixteen Polaris missiles, four 533mm (21in) torpedo tubes
POWERPLANT: one water-cooled nuclear reactor, turbines
RANGE: unlimited
PERFORMANCE: surfaced 20 knots; submerged not known 35 knots

Daphné

The Daphné class was designed in 1952 as a second-class ocean-going submarine to complement the larger Narval class. The boats were purposely designed with reduced speed in order to achieve a greater diving depth and heavier armament than was possible with the contemporary Aréthuse design of conventionally powered hunter-killer submarines. To reduce the crew's workload, the main armament was contained in 12 externally-mounted torpedo tubes, eight forward and two aft, which eliminated the need for a torpedo room and reloads. A total of 11 units was built for the French Navy. Two of the class, *Minérve* and *Eurydicé*, were lost with all hands in the western Mediterranean in 1968 and 1970 respectively. All the Daphnés had been laid up by 1990. The *Flore* went to Saudi Arabia for use as a training craft.

SPECIFICATIONS

COUNTRY: France
LAUNCH DATE: 20 June 1959
CREW: 45
DISPLACEMENT: surfaced 884 tonnes (870 tons); submerged 1062 tonnes (1045 tons)
DIMENSIONS: 58m x 7m x 4.6m (189ft 8in x 22ft 4in x 15ft 1in)
ARMAMENT: 12 552mm (21.7in) torpedo tubes
POWERPLANT: two diesels, two electric motors
RANGE: 8334km (4500nm) at 5 knots
PERFORMANCE: surfaced 13.5 knots; submerged 16 knots

DCTN F17 torpedo

The F17 was the first wire-guided torpedo to be used by the French Navy. Designed for use against surface ships from submarines, it can be employed in either the wire-guided mode or in an autonomous passive homing mode, the capability for instant switching between the two modes being provided on a control panel above the launch platform. The terminal attack phase is normally of the passive acoustic type under the torpedo's own internal control. A dual-purpose surface- or submarine-launched variant, the F17P, has been developed for the export market and has been bought by Saudi Arabia for use aboard its Madina-class frigates, and by Spain to arm its Agosta and modernized Daphne class submarines. The F17P differs from the F17 in having an active/passive acoustic homing seeker, which allows autonomous operation when required.

SPECIFICATIONS

COUNTRY: France
LAUNCH DATE: n/a
CREW: n/a
DISPLACEMENT: n/a
DIMENSIONS: 533mm x 5.9m (21in x 19.4ft)
ARMAMENT: n/a
POWERPLANT: n/a
RANGE: 18km (9.7nm)
PERFORMANCE: 35 knots

Deep Quest

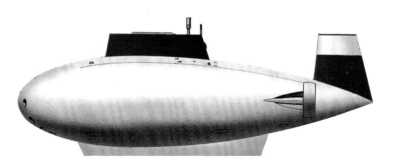

Deep Quest was the first submersible built with a fairing around a double sphere, one for the crew, the other for the propulsion unit. She works as a deep search and recovery submarine, and can descend down to 2438m (8000ft). Even the most advanced military submarines go down no further than 900m (2953ft). The pressure is crushing: 60 atmospheres at 600m (1969ft), reaching 500 on the mid-ocean bed. Pressure can exceed 1000 atmospheres in the deepest trenches: a force of almost 1100kg/m^2 (15,646lb/m^2). Vessels such as Deep Quest are vital when surveying the sea bed for cable-laying and pipeline operations. A famous vessel of similar age and type is the Alvin. It was brought to public attention in 1966 when it located and helped retrieve an H-bomb lost in the Mediterranean during World War II, when a B-52 bomber crashed.

SPECIFICATIONS

COUNTRY: United States
LAUNCH DATE: June 1967
CREW: 1–3
DISPLACEMENT: surfaced 5 tonnes (5 tons); submerged not known
DIMENSIONS: 12m (39ft 4in)
ARMAMENT: none
POWERPLANT: twin reversible thrust motors
RANGE: not known
PERFORMANCE: surfaced 4.5 knots; submerged not known

Deepstar 4000

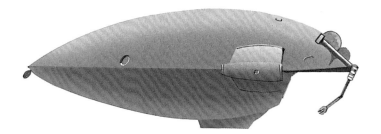

The *Deepstar 4000* was built between 1962 and 1964 by the Westinghouse Electric Corporation and the Jacques Cousteau group OFRS. The hull consists of a steel sphere with 11 openings, and she carries a wide range of scientific equipment. Pioneer vessels such as *Deepstar 4000* have lead to the discovery of hydrothermal vents, and entirely new species and ecosystems on the ocean floor. Technology has always limited the depth to which a manned submersible can operate and, during the 1980s and 1990s, great progress was made in the development of automatic or robotic deep-sea vehicles. At the turn of the twenty-first century, however, manned submersibles were increasing in their scope. The United States has developed *Deep Flight*, which is a torpedo-shaped probe designed to take one man to the bottom of the Pacific Ocean.

SPECIFICATIONS

COUNTRY: France
LAUNCH DATE: 1965
CREW: 1
DISPLACEMENT: not known
DIMENSIONS: 5.4m x 3.5m x 2m (17ft 9in x 11ft 6in x 6ft 6in)
ARMAMENT: none
POWERPLANT: two fixed, reversible 5hp AC motors
RANGE: not known
PERFORMANCE: surfaced 3 knots; submerged not known

Delta I

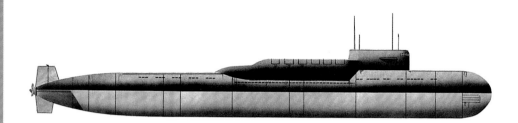

Until the early 1970s, the US led the world in highly sophisticated and effective nuclear-missile submarines. Then the Russians deployed a new class of ballistic-missile submarine, the Delta I, or Murena-class SSBN, which was a major improvement on the earlier Yankee class and which was armed with missiles that could outrange the American *Poseidon*. Each boat was armed with 12 two-stage SS-N-8 missiles. The first Delta was laid down at Severodvinsk in 1969, launched in 1971 and completed in the following year. The first of the class was paid off in 1992, three in 1993, six in 1994, one in 1995, two in 1996 and one in 1997. The remaining four boats, three of which were based with the Northern Fleet at Ostrovny and one in the Pacific at Petropavlovsk, were scheduled for withdrawal in 1999.

SPECIFICATIONS

COUNTRY: Russia
LAUNCH DATE: 1971
CREW: 120
DISPLACEMENT: submerged 11,176 tonnes (11,000 tons)
DIMENSIONS: 150m x 12m x 10.2m (492ft 1in x 39ft 4in x 33ft 6in)
ARMAMENT: 12 missile tubes, six 457mm (18in) torpedo tubes
POWERPLANT: nuclear, two reactors
RANGE: unlimited
PERFORMANCE: surfaced 19 knots; submerged 25 knots

Delta III

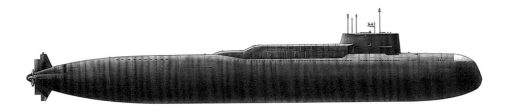

The Delta III or Kalmar-class SSBN, completed between 1976 and 1982, has some visible differences from the earlier Delta II class from which it has evolved, the most noticeable being that the missile casing is higher in order to accommodate the SS-N-18 missiles, which are longer than the SS-N-8s of the Delta II class. The last of the class is the *Delta IV*, construction of which was first ordered in December 1975. The first of eight boats was launched and commissioned in 1984 at Severodvinsk and the programme was completed in late 1990. Names are being allocated to the Delta IVs; *Kareliya* and *Novo Moskovsk* have been identified so far. Larger than the Delta III, the Delta IV is a new class of submarine, which has been given the name *Delfin* (*Dolfin*); its bases are at Saida Guba with the Northern Fleet and Rybachy in the Pacific. The first Delta IIIs paid off in 1996.

SPECIFICATIONS

COUNTRY: Russia
LAUNCH DATE: 1976
CREW: 130
DISPLACEMENT: surfaced 10,719 tonnes (10,550 tons); submerged 13,463 tonnes (13,250)
DIMENSIONS: 160m x 12m x 8.7m (524ft 11in x 39ft 4in x 28ft 5in)
ARMAMENT: 16 SS-N-18 missiles; four 533mm (21in) torpedo tubes
POWERPLANT: nuclear; two pressurized water reactors, turbines
RANGE: unlimited
PERFORMANCE: surfaced 14 knots; submerged 24 knots

Diablo

Diablo was a double-hulled ocean-going submarine developed from the previous Gato class, but was more strongly built with an improved internal layout, which increased the displacement by about 40 tonnes (39 tons). She belonged to the Tench class of 50 boats, many of which were cancelled when it was realized that the Pacific war was drawing to an end. *Diablo* did not see action during World War II. In 1964, after an extensive overhaul and refit, she was transferred on loan to Pakistan from the US Navy and renamed *Ghazi*, which means Defender of the Faith. She was sunk during the 1971 war between India and Pakistan. In addition to *Ghazi*, the Pakistan Navy possessed three French Daphné-class submarines during this period; these were the *Hangor*, *Mangro* and *Shushuk*.

SPECIFICATIONS

COUNTRY: United States
LAUNCH DATE: 30 November 1944
CREW: 85
DISPLACEMENT: surfaced 1890 tonnes (1860 tons); submerged 2467 tonnes (2420 tons)
DIMENSIONS: 93.6m x 8.3m x 4.6m (307ft 1in x 27ft 3in x 15ft 3in)
ARMAMENT: ten 533mm (21in) torpedo tubes; two 150mm (5.9in) guns
POWERPLANT: twin screw diesel engines, electric motors
RANGE: 22,518km (12,152nm) at 10 knots
PERFORMANCE: surfaced 20 knots; submerged 10 knots

Dolfijn

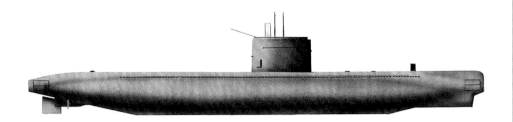

Dolfijn was one of four diesel-electric submarines completed for the Royal Netherlands Navy in the early 1960s. She was of a triple-hulled design with a maximum diving depth of nearly 304m (1000ft). Her design represented a unique solution to the problem of internal space, the hull consisting of three cylinders arranged in a triangular shape. The upper cylinder housed the crew, navigational equipment and armament, while the lower cylinders housed the machinery. Construction of the four submarines was actually authorized in 1949, but construction of two of them was suspended for some years because of financial constraints. *Dolfijn* and *Zeehond* were laid down in December 1954, *Potvis* in September 1962 and *Tonijn* November 1962. *Dolfijn* replaced another boat of the same name, which had a distinguished career in World War II.

SPECIFICATIONS

COUNTRY: Netherlands
LAUNCH DATE: 20 May 1959
CREW: 64
DISPLACEMENT: surfaced 1518 tonnes (1494 tons); submerged 1855 tonnes (1826 tons)
DIMENSIONS: 80m x 8m x 4.8m (260ft 10in x 25ft 9in x 15ft 9in)
ARMAMENT: eight 533mm (21in) torpedo tubes
POWERPLANT: twin screw diesels; two electric motors
RANGE: not known
PERFORMANCE: surfaced 14.5 knots; submerged 17 knots

Doris

Doris was the third vessel of the Daphné class designed in 1952 to complement the larger Narval class. The design uses the double-hull construction technique with the accommodation spaces split evenly fore and aft of the sail, below which is the operations and attack centre. Crew reductions were made possible by the adoption of a modular replacement system for onboard maintenance. Of the 11 units built for France, two – *Minérve* in 1968 and *Eurydicé* in 1970 – were lost with all hands while operating in the Mediterranean. The remaining boats all underwent an electronics and weapons modernization from 1970 onwards. Four units were sold to Pakistan and, in 1971, the Pakistani submarine *Hangor* sank the Indian navy frigate *Khukri* during the Indo-Pakistan War. This was the first submarine attack since World War II.

SPECIFICATIONS

COUNTRY: France
LAUNCH DATE: 20 June 1959
CREW: 45
DISPLACEMENT: surfaced 884 tonnes (870 tons); submerged 1062 tonnes (1045 tons)
DIMENSIONS: 58m x 7m x 4.6m (189ft 8in x 22ft 4in x 15ft)
ARMAMENT: 12 552mm (21.7in) torpedo tubes
POWERPLANT: two diesels, two electric motors
RANGE: 8334km (4500nm) at 5 knots
PERFORMANCE: surfaced 13.5 knots; submerged 16 knots

Dreadnought

Launched on Trafalgar Day, 21 October 1960, HMS *Dreadnought* was the Royal Navy's first nuclear-powered attack submarine (SSN), and was specifically designed to hunt and destroy hostile undersea craft. She was powered by an American S5W reactor, which was also used in the US Navy's Skipjack-class nuclear submarines; subsequent Royal Navy SSNs had British-designed nuclear plant. *Dreadnought* began sea trials in 1962. The Royal Navy carried out much pioneering work with *Dreadnought*, including proving the concept of using nuclear submarines to act as escorts for a fast carrier task group; the results of this work were made available to the US Navy, which had a close relationship with the Royal Navy at this time. Although used as a trials vessel, *Dreadnought* was a fully-capable SSN.

SPECIFICATIONS

COUNTRY: United Kingdom
LAUNCH DATE: 21 October 1960
CREW: 88
DISPLACEMENT: surfaced 3556 tonnes (3500 tons); submerged 4064 tonnes (4000 tons)
DIMENSIONS: 81m x 9.8m x 8m (265ft 9in x 32ft 3in x 26ft 3in)
ARMAMENT: six 533mm (21in) torpedo tubes
POWERPLANT: single screw, nuclear reactor, steam turbines
RANGE: unlimited
PERFORMANCE: surfaced 20 knots; submerged 30 knots

Drum

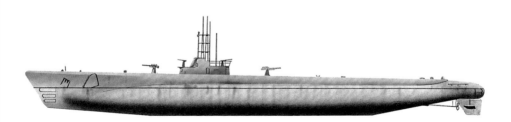

Drum was a double hull, ocean-going submarine with good seakeeping qualities and range. She was one of the Gato class of over 300 boats and, as such, was part of the largest warship project undertaken by the US Navy. These boats, more than any others, were to wreak havoc on Japan's mercantile shipping in the Pacific war. During her first offensive patrol in April 1942, Drum (under Lt Cdr Rice) sank the seaplane carrier *Mizuho* and two merchant ships, and later in the year she carried out vital reconnaissance work prior to the American landings in Guadalcanal. In October 1942, Drum sank three more ships off the east coast of Japan, and in December she torpedoed the Japanese carrier *Ryuho*. She sank a further two ships in April 1943, another in September, one in November, and three in October 1944, with another damaged. She is now a museum exhibit.

SPECIFICATIONS

COUNTRY: United States
LAUNCH DATE: 12 May 1941
CREW: 80
DISPLACEMENT: surfaced 1854 tonnes (1825 tons); submerged 2448 tonnes (2410 tons)
DIMENSIONS: 95m x 8.3m x 4.6m (311ft 9in x 27ft 3in x 15ft 3in)
ARMAMENT: ten 533mm (21in) torpedo tubes; one 76mm (3in) gun
POWERPLANT: twin screw diesels, electric motors
RANGE: 22236km (12,000nm) at 10 knots
PERFORMANCE: surfaced 20 knots; submerged 10 knots

DTCN L5 torpedo

The electrically powered L5 torpedo is available in several versions. The dual-purpose ASW/Anti-ship L5 Mod 1 is carried by surface ships, while the heavier L5 Mod 3 is used by submarines. A single-role variant, the *L5* Mod 4, was derived from the Mod 1 and is used only by surface vessels. A further version of this has been developed for the export market as the L5 Mod 4P multi-role torpedo. All versions are fitted with a Thomson-CSF active/passive guidance system and are capable of various attack profiles, including direct and programmed searches, using either of the acoustic homing techniques available. An earlier version, the L4, is used by aircraft and helicopters. The L5 and L4 were both preceded by the L3 ship- or submarine-launched ASW homing heavyweight torpedo.

SPECIFICATIONS

COUNTRY: France
LAUNCH DATE: n/a
CREW: n/a
DISPLACEMENT: n/a
DIMENSIONS: 533mm x 4.4m (21in x 14.44in)
ARMAMENT: n/a
POWERPLANT: n/a
RANGE: 9.25km (5nm)
PERFORMANCE: 35 knots

Enrico Tazzoli

Enrico Tazzoli was formerly the US submarine *Barb*, completed in 1943 as one of the vast World War II Gato class. She transferred to the Italian Navy in 1955 after conversion to the Guppy snorkel, which included a modified structure and 'fairwater' for better underwater performance. She carried 254 tonnes (250 tons) of fuel oil, enough for 19,311km (10,409nm) at 10 knots. The Italian Navy operated a number of former US Navy oceangoing submarines at this time; the others were the *Alfredo Cappellini* (ex-USS *Capitaine*); *Evangelista Torricelli* (ex-USS *Lizardfish*); *Francesco Morosini* (ex-USS *Besugo*); and *Leonardo da Vinci*, (ex-USS *Dace*). The *Tazzoli* and *da Vinci*, both of which were on extended loan from the USA, formed the backbone of the Italian submarine fleet during this period.

SPECIFICATIONS

COUNTRY: Italy
LAUNCH DATE: 02 April 1942
CREW: 80
DISPLACEMENT: surfaced 1845 tonnes (1816 tons); submerged 2463 tonnes (2425 tons)
DIMENSIONS: 94m x 8.2m x 5m (311ft 3in x 27ft x 16ft) 5in
ARMAMENT: ten 533mm (21in) torpedo tubes
POWERPLANT: twin screw diesels, electric motors
RANGE: 19,311km (10,409nm) at 10 knots
PERFORMANCE: surfaced 20 knots; submerged 10 knots

Enrico Toti

Enrico Toti was the lead boat in a class of four which were the first submarines to be built in Italy since World War II. The design was revised several times, and a coastal hunter-killer type intended for shallow and confined waters was finally approved. For these operations, the boats' relatively small size and minimum sonar cross-section were a great advantage. The main armament carried was the Whitehead Motofides A184 wire-guided torpedo; this was a dual ASW/anti-ship weapon with an active/passive acoustic homing head that featured enhanced ECCM to counter enemy decoys. With a range in the order of 25km (13.5nm), the weapon would have proved effective in an ambush situation at natural 'choke points' against much larger opponents such as Russian SSNs or SSGNs.

SPECIFICATIONS

COUNTRY: Italy
LAUNCH DATE: 12 March 1967
CREW: 26
DISPLACEMENT: surfaced 532 tonnes (524 tons); submerged 591 tonnes (582 tons)
DIMENSIONS: 46.2m x 4.7m x 4m (151ft 7in x 15ft 5in x 13ft 2in)
ARMAMENT: four 533mm (21in) torpedo tubes
POWERPLANT: single screw diesel engine, electric motors
RANGE: 5556km (3000nm) at 5 knots
PERFORMANCE: surfaced 14 knots; submerged 15 knots

Entemedor

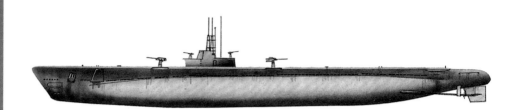

Formerly named the *Chickwick*, *Entemedor* was a double-hulled, ocean-going submarine of the large World War II Gato class. Fuel tanks, containing up to 480 tonnes (472 tons) were situated in the central double hull section. Maximum diving depth was 95m (312ft). *Entemedor* was transferred to Turkey in 1973. During the years of the Cold War, Turkey – a vital component of NATO's Southern Flank – had a navy that was an extraordinary collection of obsolescent American warships. In the late 1960s it included ten submarines of the Gato class, all of which had been loaned by the US under the terms of the NATO Mutual Assistance Pact. All had been modified to carry up-to-date equipment, including the 'guppy snorkel' in some cases. The *Entemedor* was named *Preveze* in Turkish service. The development of the Turkish navy has mirrored that of Greece, its main rival.

SPECIFICATIONS

COUNTRY: Turkey
LAUNCH DATE: 17 December 1944
CREW: 80
DISPLACEMENT: surfaced 1854 tonnes (1825 tons); submerged 2458 tonnes (2420 tons)
DIMENSIONS: 95m x 8.3m x 4.6m (311ft 9in x 27ft 3in x 15ft 3in)
ARMAMENT: ten 533mm (21in) torpedo tubes; one 127mm (5in) gun
POWERPLANT: twin screw diesel engines, electric motors
RANGE: 20,372km (11,000nm) at 10 knots
PERFORMANCE: surfaced 20 knots; submerged 8.7 knots

Evangelista Torricelli

Evangelista Torricelli was formerly the US ocean-going submarine *Lizardfish* of the vast Gato class, and was originally to have been named *Luigi Torelli*. She was handed over to Italy on 5 March 1966, along with two sister vessels, the *Alfredo Cappellini* (ex-USS *Capitaine*) and *Francesco Morosini* (ex-USS *Besugo*). The United States supplied many former Gato-class submarines to its Allies in the years of the Cold War; all had their 100mm (3.9in) guns removed and were upgraded. Their long range and reliability made them very attractive vessels, as indeed did their war record in the Pacific, which was outstanding. The *Morosini* was the first to be discarded, in November 1975, followed by the *Toricelli* in 1976 and the *Cappellini* in 1977. *Toricelli* was used for experimental work in her latter years.

SPECIFICATIONS

COUNTRY: Italy
LAUNCH DATE: July 1944
CREW: 85
DISPLACEMENT: surfaced 1845 tonnes (1816 tons); submerged 2463 tonnes (2425 tons)
DIMENSIONS: 95m x 8.2m x 5m (311ft 6in x 27ft x 16ft 5in)
ARMAMENT: ten 533mm (21in) torpedo tubes
POWERPLANT: twin screw diesel engines, electric motors
RANGE: 22,518km (12,152nm) at 10 knots
PERFORMANCE: surfaced 20 knots; submerged 10 knots

Explorer

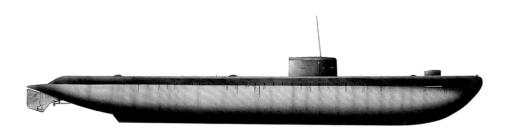

Explorer and her sister *Excalibur* were two experimental submarines ordered from Vickers-Armstrong by the Royal Navy. The streamlined hull was designed to operate at high underwater speeds, which were made possible by using high test peroxide similar to that used in the effective German type XXI submarines built towards the end of World War II. *Explorer* was the first submarine to be launched for the Royal Navy since the completion of the A class of 1948. The vessels yielded much valuable data on future hull design connected with the UK's first-generation nuclear submarines, which were then at the initial concept phase; work on the design of the first American and Russian nuclear submarines was already well advanced in 1954, when the experimental British craft were launched.

SPECIFICATIONS

COUNTRY: United Kingdom
LAUNCH DATE: March 1954
CREW: 70
DISPLACEMENT: surfaced 792 tonnes (780 tons); submerged 1016 tonnes (1000 tons)
DIMENSIONS: 68.7m x 4.8m x 5.5m (225ft 5in x 15ft 8in x 18ft 2in)
ARMAMENT: none
POWERPLANT: twin screw diesel engines, hydrogen peroxide
RANGE: not known
PERFORMANCE: surfaced 20 knots; submerged 25 knots

FFV Tp42 series

The Swedish Tp42 is the base model for a whole series of lightweight torpedoes built by FFV for the home market and for export. The basic model, the Tp422, entered service in mid-1983 and is intended primarily for ASW operations from the Swedish Navy's small helicopter fleet. It was the first western torpedo to be capable of wire guidance after an an air-launched delivery. Propulsion is by an electric battery of the silver-zinc type, and the warhead is fitted with both proximity and contact fuses. The torpedo can be set to run at one of two speeds which are changeable after launch either via the guidance wire or as an instruction pre-programmed into the seeker unit. Later variants use digital micro-processor guidance units and are optimized to attack the latest generation of quiet conventional submarines (SSKs) operating in shallow waters.

SPECIFICATIONS
COUNTRY: Sweden
LAUNCH DATE: n/a
CREW: n/a
DISPLACEMENT: n/a
DIMENSIONS: 400mm x 2.44m (15.75in x 8ft)
ARMAMENT: n/a
POWERPLANT: n/a
RANGE: 20km (10.8nm)
PERFORMANCE: 15–25 knots

FFV Tp61 series

Designed by FFV for use against surface ship targets, the Tp61 entered service in 1967 as a non-terminal-homing wire-guided heavyweight torpedo for use by surface ships, submarines and coastal defence batteries. In 1984, the longer-range Tp613 entered service as the Tp61's successor with essentially the same propulsion system and a terminal homing seeker that utilizes an onboard computer to oversee the attack and, if necessary, to initiate previously programmed search patterns at the target's predicted location. The torpedo's thermal propulsion system combines hydrogen peroxide with ethanol to power a 12-cylinder steam motor which produces an almost invisible wake signature. Compared with modern electrically powered weapons at similar speed, the maximum range attainable is three to five times greater.

SPECIFICATIONS
COUNTRY: Sweden
LAUNCH DATE: n/a
CREW: n/a
DISPLACEMENT: n/a
DIMENSIONS: 533m x 7m (21in x 23ft)
ARMAMENT: n/a
POWERPLANT: n/a
RANGE: 20km (10.8nm)
PERFORMANCE: 45 knots

Flutto

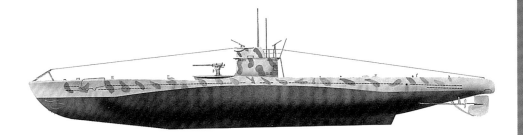

Flutto was one of a class of medium submarines planned in three groups, all to be completed by the end of 1944. In the end only eight of the first group were finished. Two of the class, *Grongo* and *Merena*, were each fitted with four cylinders for the transport of human torpedoes. Of those that did become operational, *Tritone* was sunk off Bougie on 19 January 1943, by gunfire from the British destroyer *Antelope* and the Canadian corvette *Port Arthur*; *Gorgo* was sunk off the Algerian coast by the American destroyer USS *Nields* on 21 May 1943; and *Flutto* was sunk off the coast of Sicily on 11 July 1943, by the British motor torpedo boats 640, 651 and 670. *Nautilo*, sunk in an air raid and refloated, was assigned to the Yugoslav Navy and renamed *Sava*; and *Marea* went to Russia as the *Z13*.

SPECIFICATIONS

COUNTRY: Italy
LAUNCH DATE: November 1942
CREW: 50
DISPLACEMENT: surfaced 973 tonnes (958 tons); submerged 1189 tonnes (1170 tons)
DIMENSIONS: 63.2m x 7m x 4.9m (207ft 4in x 23ft x 16ft 1in)
ARMAMENT: six 533mm (21in) torpedo tubes, one 100mm (3.9in) gun
POWERPLANT: twin screw diesel engines, electric motors
RANGE: 10,000km (5400nm) at 8 knots
PERFORMANCE: surfaced 16 knots; submerged 7 knots

Foxtrot class

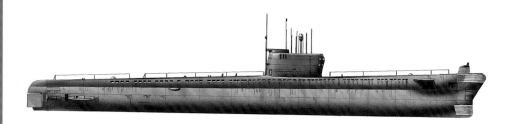

Built in the periods 1958–68 (45 units) and 1971–74 (17 units), the Foxtrot-class diesel-electric submarine remained in production at a slow rate for export, the last unit being launched in 1984. The class proved to be the most successful of the post-war Russian conventional submarine designs, 62 serving with the former Soviet Navy. Three Soviet Navy Fleet Areas operated Foxtrot, and the Mediterranean and Indian Ocean Squadrons regularly had these boats deployed to them. The Foxtrots were used more regularly for long-range ocean patrols than Russia's SSNs. The first foreign recipient of the type was India, which received eight new boats between 1968 and 1976. India was followed by Libya, with six units received between 1976 and 1983, and Cuba, three boats being handed over between 1979 and 1984. All Russian Foxtrots were withdrawn by the late 1980s.

SPECIFICATIONS

COUNTRY: Russia
LAUNCH DATE: 1959 (first unit)
CREW: 80
DISPLACEMENT: surfaced 1950 tonnes (1919 tons); submerged 2500 tonnes (2540 tons)
DIMENSIONS: 91.5m x 8m x 6.1m (300ft 2in x 26ft 3in x 20ft)
ARMAMENT: ten 533mm (21in) torpedo tubes
POWERPLANT: three shafts, three diesel engines and three electric motors
RANGE: 10,190km (5500nm) at 8 knots
PERFORMANCE: surfaced 18 knots; submerged 16 knots

Gal

Gal is one of three German-designed Type 206 boats built by Vickers of Barrow in the UK in the mid-1970s, following a contract signed in April 1972. *Gal*, laid down in 1973 and commissioned in December 1976, ran aground on her delivery voyage, but was repaired. The other two boats, *Tanin* and *Rahav*, were commissioned in June and December 1977 respectively. The Type 206 is a development of the Type 205; built of high tensile non-magnetic steel, it was intended for coastal operations and had to conform with treaty limitations on the maximum tonnage allowed for West Germany. New safety devices for the crew were fitted, and the weapons fit allowed for the carriage of wire-guided torpedoes. The Type 206 was just one of a range of similar boats offered for export.

SPECIFICATIONS

COUNTRY: Israel
LAUNCH DATE: 2 December 1975
CREW: 22
DISPLACEMENT: surfaced 427 tonnes (420 tons); submerged 610 tonnes (600 tons)
DIMENSIONS: 45m x 4.7m x 3.7m (147ft 8in x 15ft 5in x 12ft 2in)
ARMAMENT: eight 533mm (21in) torpedo tubes
POWERPLANT: single shaft, two diesels, one electric motor
RANGE: 7038km (3800nm) at 10 knots
PERFORMANCE: surfaced 11 knots; submerged 17 knots

Galerna

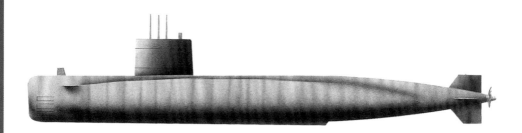

Galerna was a medium-range submarine built to the design of the French Agosta class. She marked a major step forward in Spanish submarine technology. This submarine and her three sisters can carry 16 reload torpedoes or nine torpedoes and 19 mines. A full sonar kit is carried, comprising one active and one passive set. The first two boats, *Galerna* and *Siroco*, were ordered in May 1975, and a second pair (*Mistral* and *Tramontana*) in June 1977. The Spanish Agosta class boats are armed with four bow torpedo tubes, which are fitted with a rapid-reload pneumatic ramming system that can launch the weapons quickly but with a minimum of noise. The boats have a diving depth of 350m (1148ft). They were built with some French help, and were all upgraded in the mid-1990s.

SPECIFICATIONS

COUNTRY: Spain
LAUNCH DATE: 5 December 1981
CREW: 54
DISPLACEMENT: surfaced 1473 tonnes (1450 tons); submerged 1753 tonnes (1725 tons)
DIMENSIONS: 67.6m x 6.8m x 5.4m (221ft 9in x 22ft 4in x 17ft 9in)
ARMAMENT: four 551mm (21.7in) torpedo tubes
POWERPLANT: single screw diesel/electric motors
RANGE: 13,672km (7378nm) at 9 knots
PERFORMANCE: surfaced 12 knots; submerged 20 knots

George Washington

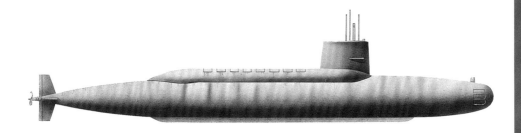

In 1955, the Soviet Union began modifying six existing diesel submarines to carry nuclear-tipped ballistic missiles. America was simultaneously developing the Jupiter missile, which was to equip a projected 10,160-tonne (10,000-ton) nuclear submarine. Jupiter used a mix of highly volatile liquids for its propellant, and was posing immense problems of safety and operation. The smaller, lighter Polaris A1 presented a more suitable alternative. The nuclear submarine *Scorpion*, then being built, was chosen as the delivery platform for the new weapon and a new 40m (13ft) hull section was added just aft of the conning tower to house 16 missiles in vertical launch tubes. Renamed *George Washington*, she was the first of a new type of weapons platform, and put the US far ahead in the nuclear arms race.

SPECIFICATIONS

COUNTRY: United States
LAUNCH DATE: June 1959
CREW: 112
DISPLACEMENT: surfaced 6115 tonnes (6019 tons); submerged 6998 tonnes (6888 tons)
DIMENSIONS: 116.3m x 10m x 8.8m (381ft 7in x 32ft 10in x 28ft 10in)
ARMAMENT: 16 Polaris missiles, six 533mm (21in) torpedo tubes
POWERPLANT: single screw, one pressurized water-cooled reactor, turbines
RANGE: unlimited
PERFORMANCE: surfaced 20 knots; submerged 30.5 knots

George Washington Carver

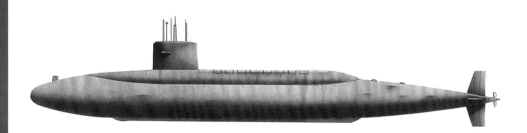

George Washington Carver was one of 29 vessels of the Lafayette class, enlarged versions of the Ethan Allen class, and all were refitted with Poseidon missiles. She was laid down in April 1964 and was completed in August 1966. This class of submarine could dive to depths of up to 300m (985ft) and the nuclear reactor core provided enough energy to propel the vessel for 760,000km (347,200nm), which, to all intents and purposes, gave it an unlimited endurance. Like all American SSBNs, George Washington Carver had two crews which carried out alternate 68-day patrols, with 32-day refit periods between patrols. The vessels underwent an extensive refit, which took nearly two years to complete, every six years in rotation. George Washington Carver was deactivated on 2 November 1992.

SPECIFICATIONS

COUNTRY: United States
LAUNCH DATE: 14 August 1965
CREW: 140
DISPLACEMENT: surfaced 7366 tonnes (7250 tons); submerged 8382 tonnes (8250 tons)
DIMENSIONS: 129.5m x 10m x 9.6m (424ft 10in x 32ft 10in x 31ft 10in)
ARMAMENT: 16 Trident C4 missiles, four 533mm (21in) torpedo tubes
POWERPLANT: single screw, one pressurized water-cooled nuclear reactor
RANGE: unlimited
PERFORMANCE: surfaced 20 knots; submerged 30 knots

Giuliano Prini

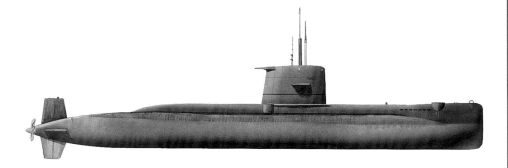

The *Giuliano Prini* is one of four SSKs laid down by Fincantieri, Monfalcone, for the Italian Navy between 1984 and 1992. The first two boats, *Salvatore Pelosi* and *Giuliano Prini*, were ordered in March 1983 and the second pair, *Primo Longobardo* and *Gianfranco Gazzana Priaroggia*, in July 1988. The latter two boats have a slightly longer hull to provide space for the installation of SSMs, and the possibility of installing either Exocet or Harpoon was still being discussed in 1999. Test diving depth of the class is 300m (985ft) and the hull structure can withstand pressures down to 600m (1970ft) before crushing. The boats have an operational endurance of 45 days and a submerged range of 402km (217nm) at 4 knots. The SSK is a vital component of Italy's naval inventory because of the need to protect the country's long coastline from infiltration.

SPECIFICATIONS

COUNTRY: Italy
LAUNCH DATE: 12 December 1987
CREW: 50
DISPLACEMENT: surfaced 1500 tonnes (1476 tons); submerged 1689 tonnes (1662 tons)
DIMENSIONS: 64.4m x 6.8m x 5.6m (211ft 2in x 22ft 3in x 18ft 5in)
ARMAMENT: six 533mm (21in) torpedo tubes
POWERPLANT: single shaft, diesel/electric motors
RANGE: 17,692km (9548nm) at 11 knots
PERFORMANCE: surfaced 11 knots; submerged 19 knots

Golf I

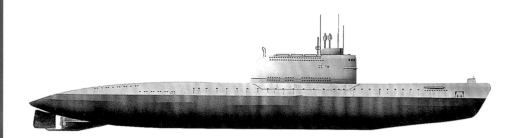

By the 1950s, Russia had embarked upon a massive submarine programme that would initially give her a larger fleet of submarines than any other country. Twenty-three Golf I-class boats were completed between 1958 and 1962, and entered service at a rate of six or seven a year. One unit was built in China from Russian-supplied components. The ballistic missiles were housed vertically in the rear section of the extended fin, which produced a great deal of resistance underwater and reduced speed, as well as generating high noise levels; however, the boats could be driven by a creep motor, giving quiet operation and very long endurance. Thirteen Golf I boats were modified to Golf II standard starting in 1965, using the SS-N-5 ballistic missile. Code-named Sark by NATO, this was a single-stage, liquid-fuelled missile with a range of 1400km (750nm).

SPECIFICATIONS

COUNTRY: Russia
LAUNCH DATE: 1977
CREW: 86
DISPLACEMENT: surfaced 2336 tonnes (2300 tons); submerged 2743 tonnes (2700 tons)
DIMENSIONS: 100m x 8.5m x 6.6m (328ft 1in x 27ft 11in x 21ft 8in)
ARMAMENT: three SS-N-4 ballistic missiles; ten 533mm (21in) torpedo tubes
POWERPLANT: triple screws, diesel/electric motors
RANGE: 36,510km (19,703nm) at 10 knots
PERFORMANCE: surfaced 17 knots; submerged 14 knots

Grayback

Grayback and her sister vessel, *Growler*, were originally intended to be attack submarines, but in 1956 their design was modified to provide a missile-launching capability using the Regulus, a nuclear-tipped high-altitude cruise missile which was launched by solid-fuel boosters and then guided to its target by radio command signals from the submarine, cruising at periscope depth. Both submarines were withdrawn from service in 1964, when the Regulus programme ended, but *Grayback* was subsequently converted to an Amphibious Transport Submarine (LPSS), capable of carrying 67 Marines and their assault craft. Her torpedo tubes and attack capability were retained. *Growler* was also to have been converted, but this was deferred because of rising costs. As a command ship, *Grayback* had a crew of 96 and could accommodate 10 officers and 75 men.

SPECIFICATIONS

COUNTRY: United States
LAUNCH DATE: 2 July 1957
CREW: 84
DISPLACEMENT: surfaced 2712 tonnes (2670 tons); submerged 3708 tons (3650 tons)
DIMENSIONS: 102m x 9m (335ft x 30ft)
ARMAMENT: four Regulus missiles, eight 533mm (21in) torpedo tubes
POWERPLANT: twin screws, diesel/electric motors
RANGE: 14,824km (8000nm) at 10 knots
PERFORMANCE: surfaced 20 knots; submerged 17 knots

Grongo

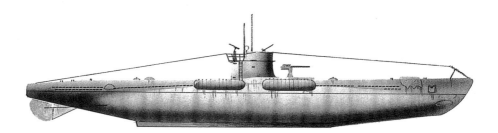

Grongo was one of the 12-strong Flutto class of submarines, among the last to be built for the Italian Navy before the Armistice with the Allied powers was concluded. The Fluttos were in turn developed from the Argo class, which had been launched in 1936. *Grongo*'s diesel engines developed 1790kW (2400hp), and surfaced range was 10,260km (5530nm) at eight knots. Her electric motors developed 597kW (800hp), and submerged range was 128km (69nm) at 4 knots or 13km (7nm) at seven knots. *Grongo* was scuttled at La Spezia in 1943, but the Germans raised her and commissioned her into the German Navy as the *UIT20*. She was sunk in a British air attack on Genoa on 4 September 1944. One of this class, *Marea*, was later transferred to Soviet Russia under the terms of the Peace Treaty and served until 1960 as the *Z13*.

SPECIFICATIONS

COUNTRY: Italy
LAUNCH DATE: 6 May 1943
CREW: 50
DISPLACEMENT: surfaced 960 tonnes (945 tons); submerged 1130 tonnes (1113 tons)
DIMENSIONS: 63m x 6.9m x 4.8m (207ft 2in x 22ft 8in x 15ft 9in)
ARMAMENT: six 533mm (21in) torpedo tubes, one 100mm (3.9in) gun
POWERPLANT: twin screws, diesel/electric motors
RANGE: 10,260km (5530nm) at 8 knots
PERFORMANCE: surfaced 16 knots; submerged 7 knots

Grouper

Grouper was originally completed as one of the Gato class, and ten years later she was converted into one of the first hunter-killer submarines (SSK) dedicated specifically to tracking down and destroying enemy submarines. The concept required that the hunter-killer submarine be very quiet and carry long-range listening sonar with high bearing accuracy. So equipped, the submarine could lie in wait off enemy bases, or in narrow straits, and intercept the enemy boats as they moved out to patrol. *Grouper* was converted in 1951, and in 1958 she became the sonar test submarine for the Underwater Sound Laboratory at New London. The work she did in this respect was vital in building up a library of underwater 'sound signatures'. The submarine was decommissioned in 1968, and was scrapped in 1970.

SPECIFICATIONS

COUNTRY: United States
LAUNCH DATE: 7 October 1941
CREW: 80
DISPLACEMENT: surfaced 1845 tonnes (1816 tons); submerged 2463 tonnes (2425 tons)
DIMENSIONS: 94.8m x 8.2m x 4.5m (311ft 3in x 27ft x 14ft 9in)
ARMAMENT: ten 533mm (21in) torpedo tubes
POWERPLANT: twin screws, diesel/electric motors
RANGE: 19,300km (10,416nm) at 10 knots
PERFORMANCE: surfaced 20.25 knots; submerged 10 knots

Ha 201 class

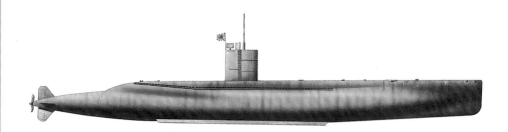

Ordered under a crash programme of 1943–44, these small submarines had a high underwater speed and excellent manoeuvrability, and were designed for the sole purpose of defending the Japanese Home Islands against American warships. Large numbers were planned, and it was hoped that the production schedule could be met by prefabricating parts of the hull in the workshops and assembling them on the slipway. Electric welding was extensively used, and the first unit, *Ha 201*, was laid down in the Sasebo Naval Yard on 1 May 1945 and completed on 31 May 1945. Owing to the critical shortage of materials and to American bombing, only 10 units had been completed by the end of the war, and none carried out any active patrols. *Ha 201* was scuttled by the US Navy in April 1946.

SPECIFICATIONS

COUNTRY: Japan
LAUNCH DATE: May 1945
CREW: 22
DISPLACEMENT: surfaced 383 tonnes (377 tons); submerged 447 tonnes (440 tons)
DIMENSIONS: 50m x 3.9m x 3.4m (164ft 1in x 12ft 10in x 11ft 3in)
ARMAMENT: two 533mm (21in) torpedo tubes; one 7.7mm AA gun
POWERPLANT: single shaft diesel/electric motor
RANGE: 5559km (3000nm) at 10 knots
PERFORMANCE: surfaced 10.5 knots; submerged 13 knots

Hai Lung

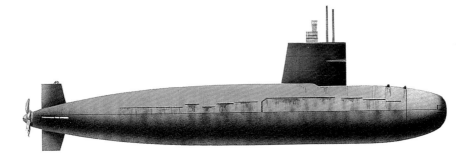

The Taiwanese Navy was set up in the 1950s to counter the threat of invasion from mainland China. Two of its most modern and effective warships are the diesel-electric submarines of the Hai Lung (Sea Dragon) class. They are modified Zwaardvis-class submarines purchased from Holland, which were probably the most efficient conventional submarine design of the 1970s. The Zwaardvis boats were themselves based on the US Barbel class, but had many differences in detail and equipment. *Hai Lung* and her sister *Hai Hu* were commissioned in December 1987, and were the first export orders for Dutch-built submarines. Their delivery was made in the face of strong protests from the People's Republic of China, and a further order for two boats was blocked by the Netherlands government. *Hai Lung* and *Hai Hu* underwent further equipment updates in the 1990s.

SPECIFICATIONS

COUNTRY: Taiwan
LAUNCH DATE: October 1986
CREW: 67
DISPLACEMENT: surfaced 2414 tonnes (2376 tons); submerged 2702 tonnes (2660 tons)
DIMENSIONS: 66m x 8.4m x 7.1m (216ft 6in x 27ft 7in x 23ft 4in)
ARMAMENT: six 533mm (21in) torpedo tubes
POWERPLANT: single screw, diesel/electric motors
RANGE: 19,000km (10,241nm) at 9 knots
PERFORMANCE: surfaced 11 knots; submerged 20 knots

Han

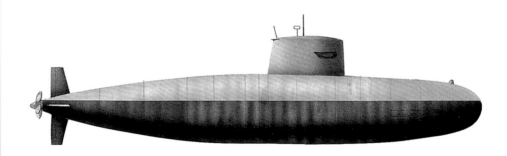

The Chinese Navy took a massive leap forward in the early 1970s with its Han-class nuclear-attack submarines (SSNs). The highly streamlined hull shape was based on the design of the USS *Albacore*, and was a radical departure from previous Chinese submarine designs. While the Russians cut many corners to get their first SSNs into service, China proceeded at a more leisurely pace, and although the Han class of four boats is fairly basic, with little of the high technology that is standard on American and British vessels, it provided a solid basis for further development. From the Hans came the Xia class, which was China's first nuclear ballistic-missile submarine. According to some reports, however, China's SSN/SSBN programme has suffered its fair share of accidents, which have been concealed from the rest of the world.

SPECIFICATIONS

COUNTRY: China
LAUNCH DATE: 1972
CREW: 120
DISPLACEMENT: surfaced not known; submerged 5080 tonnes (5000 tons)
DIMENSIONS: 90m x 8m x 8.2m (295ft 3in x 26ft 3in x 27ft)
ARMAMENT: six 533mm (21in) torpedo tubes
POWERPLANT: single screw, pressurized water nuclear reactor
RANGE: unlimited
PERFORMANCE: surfaced 20 knots; submerged 28 knots

Harpoon missile

In 1967, following the sinking of the Israeli destroyer *Eilat* by a Russian-built Styx anti-ship missile, the US Navy began to show serious interest in developing an advanced weapon of this type. The result was a formal proposal that led to the McDonnell Douglas Harpoon, a weapon that has been constantly updated over the years to match the changing threat. Harpoon, which can be launched from surface vessels, aircraft and submarines (the Sub-Harpoon version) is a highly effective weapon. Flight control is achieved by cruciform rear fins. One round is capable of destroying a guided missile boat, two will disable a frigate, four will knock out a misisile cruiser, and five will destroy a Kirov-class battlecruiser or a Kiev-class aircraft carrier. The Harpoon has been a great export success in Europe and the Middle East.

SPECIFICATIONS

COUNTRY: United States
LAUNCH DATE: n/a
CREW: n/a
DISPLACEMENT: n/a
DIMENSIONS: 343mm x 4.62m (13.5in x 15.2ft)
ARMAMENT: n/a
POWERPLANT: n/a
RANGE: 160km (86nm)
PERFORMANCE: 0.85M

H

Harushio (1967)

Harushio was one of the Japanese Maritime Self-Defence Force's five Oshio class submarines, completed in the mid-1960s. They were a large design in order to achieve improved seaworthiness and to allow the installation of more comprehensive sonar and electronic devices. They were the first Japanese submarines capable of deep diving. All five were built at Kobe, construction being shared between Kawasaki and Mitsubishi. The other boats in the class were *Oshio*, *Arashio*, *Michishio* and *Asashio*. The submarines were named after tides; *Oshio*, for example, means Flood Tide, while *Asashio* means Morning Tide. Because the lead boat, *Oshio*, had a different configuration from the others, with a larger bow and less sophisticated sonar, the boats are often cited as two separate classes.

SPECIFICATIONS

COUNTRY: Japan
LAUNCH DATE: 25 February 1967
CREW: 80
DISPLACEMENT: surfaced 1676 tonnes (1650 tons); submerged not known
DIMENSIONS: 88m x 8.2m x 4.9m (288ft 8in x 27ft x 16ft 2in)
ARMAMENT: eight 533mm (21in) torpedo tubes
POWERPLANT: two shafts, diesel/electic motors
RANGE: 16,677km (9000nm) at 10 knots
PERFORMANCE: surfaced 14 knots; submerged 18 knots

Harushio (1989)

The six submarines of the Harushio class were a natural progression from the previous Yushio class, with improved noise reduction and ZQR-1 towed array sonar. They are also equipped with the Hughes/Oki ZQQ-5B hull sonar. All five boats are capable of firing the Sub-Harpoon anti-ship missile from their torpedo tubes. Beginning with *Harushio* in 1989, the boats were built at the rate of one a year to replace the vessels of the Uzushio class. The other five boats, in order of their launch date, are named *Natsushio*, *Hayashio*, *Arashio*, *Wakashio* and *Fuyushio*. Their excellent endurance means that they can be deployed in a defensive screen well out from their home bases. The class will provide the Japanese Navy with a very effective conventional underwater attack capability until well into the twenty-first century.

SPECIFICATIONS

COUNTRY: Japan
LAUNCH DATE: 26 July 1989
CREW: 75
DISPLACEMENT: surfaced 2489 tonnes (2450 tons); submerged not known
DIMENSIONS: 77m x 10m x 7.75m (252ft 7in x 32ft 10in x 25ft 4in)
ARMAMENT: six 533mm (21in) torpedo tubes, Sub-Harpoon SSM
POWERPLANT: single shaft, diesel/electric motors
RANGE: 22,236km (12,000nm) at 10 knots
PERFORMANCE: surfaced 12 knots; submerged 20 knots

I201

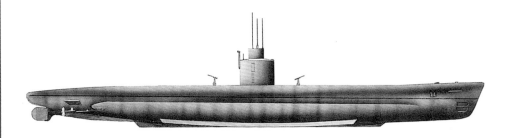

Ordered under an emergency 1943-44 construction programme, the I201 class of high-speed submarines was designed as a result of trials carried out with an experimental submarine just before World War II; they compared very favourably with the German Type XXI. They were highly streamlined, making extensive use of electric welding, and even the twin 25mm (0.98in) AA guns were on mounts that retracted into the hull. The lightweight MAN diesels contributed to a small displacement, which in turn gave rise to a fast submerged speed; the 3729kW (5000hp) electric motors could propel the boat under water at 19 knots for nearly an hour. None of the boats was able to carry out any operational patrols before the end of the war; all were scuttled by the US Navy or scrapped with the exception of *I204*, sunk in an air attack.

SPECIFICATIONS

COUNTRY: Japan
LAUNCH DATE: 1944
CREW: 100
DISPLACEMENT: surfaced 1311 tonnes (1291 tons); submerged 1473 tonnes (1450 tons)
DIMENSIONS: 79m x 5.8m x 5.4m (259ft 2in x 19ft x 17ft 9in)
ARMAMENT: four 533mm (21in) torpedo tubes
POWERPLANT: twin screws, diesel/electric motors
RANGE: 10,747km (5800nm) at 14 knots
PERFORMANCE: surfaced 15.7 knots; submerged 19 knots

I351

The three submarines of the I351 class were intended to act as supply bases for seaplanes and flying boats, for which role they were equipped to carry 396 tonnes (390 tons) of cargo, including 371 tonnes (365 tons) of petrol, 11.18 tonnes (11 tons) of fresh water and 60 250kg (550lb) bombs, or alternatively 30 bombs and 15 aircraft torpedoes. By the end of the war, only the *I351* had been completed, and she was sunk by the American submarine USS *Bluefish* on 14 July 1945, after six months in service. A second boat, the *I352*, was sunk by air attack at Kure when she was 90 per cent complete, and a third, *I353*, was never laid down, having been cancelled in 1943. *I351* had a safe diving depth of 96m (315ft) and had an underwater range of 185km (100nm) at three knots. The role of these submarines was dictated by the loss of Japan's Pacific bases.

SPECIFICATIONS

COUNTRY: Japan
LAUNCH DATE: 1944
CREW: 90
DISPLACEMENT: surfaced 3568 tonnes (3512 tons); submerged 4358 tonnes (4290 tons)
DIMENSIONS: 110m x 10.2m x 6m (361ft x 33ft 6in x 19ft 8in)
ARMAMENT: four 533mm (12in) torpedo tubes
POWERPLANT: twin screws, diesel/electric motors
RANGE: 24,076km (13,000nm) at 14 knots
PERFORMANCE: surfaced 15.8 knots; submerged 6.3 knots

I400

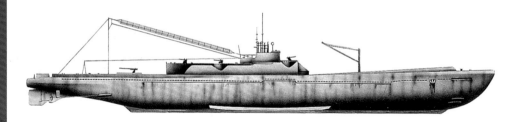

Prior to World War II, several navies tried to build an effective aircraft-carrying submarine. Only the Japanese managed to produce a series of workable vessels, the most notable being the STO class. Of the 19 planned vessels only two, the *I400* and *I401*, were completed for their intended role. A third, *I402*, was completed as a submersible tanker transport. *I400* was a huge vessel, with a large aircraft hangar offset to starboard, to hold three M6A1 Seiran floatplanes, plus components for a fourth. To launch the aircraft, *I400* would surface, then the machines would be warmed up in the hangar, rolled out, wings unfolded and launched down a 26m (85ft) catapult rail. It was planned to attack the locks on the Panama Canal, but the mission was never flown. The I400 class was not rivalled in size until the emergence of the Ethan Allen class of SSBN.

SPECIFICATIONS

COUNTRY: Japan
LAUNCH DATE: 1944
CREW: 100
DISPLACEMENT: surfaced 5316 tonnes (5233 tons); submerged 6665 tonnes (6560 tons)
DIMENSIONS: 122m x 12m x 7m (400ft 1in x 39ft 4in x 24ft)
ARMAMENT: eight 533mm (21in) torpedo tubes; one 140mm (5.5in) gun
POWERPLANT: twin screws, diesel/electric motors
RANGE: 68,561km (37,000nm) at 14 knots
PERFORMANCE: aurfaced: 18.7 knots; submerged 6.5 knots

India

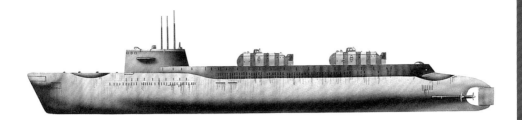

IndiaI *ndia* was designed for salvage and
rescue operations. Her hull was built
for high surface speeds, enabling her
to be deployed rapidly to her rescue
coordinates. Two rescue submarines are
carried in semi-recessed deck wells aft,
and personnel can enter the mother boat
from these when she is submerged. The
boat can also operate under ice. India-
class submarines are believed to operate
in support of Russian Spetsnaz special
operations brigades when not being used
in their primary role, carrying two IRM
amphibious reconnaissance vehicles;
these are capable of travelling along the
sea bed on tracks as well as operating
in thenormal swimming mode. Two
Indias were built, and deployed with the
Northern and Pacific Fleets. They have
been observed going to the aid of Russian
nuclear submarines involved in accidents.

SPECIFICATIONS
COUNTRY: Russia
LAUNCH DATE: 1979
CREW: 70 (plus accommodation for 120 others)
DISPLACEMENT: surfaced 3251 tonnes (3200 tons);
submerged 4064 tonnes (4000 tons)
DIMENSIONS: 106m x 10m (347ft 9in x 32ft 10in)
ARMAMENT: four 533mm (21in) torpedo tubes
POWERPLANT: twin screws, diesel/electric motors
RANGE: not known
PERFORMANCE: surfaced 15 knots; submerged
10 knots

K

Kilo class

Built at the river shipyard of Komsomolsk in the Russian Far East, the first medium-range Kilo-class submarine was launched early in 1980. By 1982, construction had also started at the Gorki shipyard, while export production began in 1985 at Sudomekh. In August 1985, the first operational Kilo deployed to the vast Vietnamese naval base at Cam Ranh Bay for weapon systems trials under tropical conditions, and in the following year the first sighting of a Kilo in the Indian Ocean was made by a warship of the Royal Australian Navy. The Kilo class has a more advanced hull form than the other contemporary Russian conventional submarine designs, and is more typical of western 'teardrop' submarine hulls. Fifteen Kilos were still in Russian service in 1998, and Kilo production continues at the rate of two a year for export.

SPECIFICATIONS

COUNTRY: Russia
LAUNCH DATE: early 1980 (first unit)
CREW: 45–50
DISPLACEMENT: surfaced 2494 tonnes (2455 tons); submerged 3193 tonnes (3143 tons)
DIMENSIONS: 69m x 9m x 7m (226ft 5in x 29ft 6in x 23ft)
ARMAMENT: six 533mm (21in) torpedo tubes
POWERPLANT: single shaft, three diesels, three electric motors
RANGE: 11,112km (6000nm) at 7 knots
PERFORMANCE: surfaced 15 knots; submerged 24 knots

Le Terrible

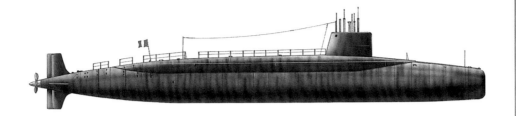

Laid down at Cherbourg Naval Dockyard on 24 June 1967, *Le Terrible* was the third unit of France's Redoutable-class nuclear ballistic-missile submarines. forming the seaborne element of the French Force de Dissuasion (Deterrent Force), which ultimately consisted of boats armed with the MSBS (Mer-Sol Ballistique Strategique) IRBM. The French term for SSBN is SNLE (Sous-marin Nucléaire Lance-Engins). The *Redoutable* reached IOC in December 1971; *Le Terrible* followed in 1973, *Le Foudroyant* in 1974, *Indomptable* in 1977 and *Le Tonnant* in 1979. The first operational launch of an M4, which can be discharged rapidly, was made by *Le Tonnant* on 15 September 1987 in the Atlantic. The *Redoutable* was withdrawn in 1991; two other boats, *Indomptable* and *Le Tonnant*, were upgraded and assigned to the Inflexible class.

SPECIFICATIONS

COUNTRY: France
LAUNCH DATE: 12 December 1969
CREW: 114
DISPLACEMENT: surfaced 7620 tonnes (7500 tons); submerged 9144 tons (9000 tons)
DIMENSIONS: 128m x 10.6m x 10m (420ft x 34ft 10in x 32ft 10in)
ARMAMENT: 16 submarine-launched MRBMs
POWERPLANT: one nuclear PWR, turbines
RANGE: unlimited
PERFORMANCE: surfaced 20 knots; submerged 28 knots

Le Triomphant

Le Triomphant is leader of the latest class of French nuclear-powered ballistic-missile submarines, all built by DCN Cherbourg. She was ordered on 10 March 1986 and floated in dock in November 1993. The second, *Le Téméraire*, was ordered on 18 October 1989 and launched on 8 August 1997, while the third, *Le Vigilant*, ordered on 27 May 1993, is scheduled to be launched in May 2002. A fourth vessel, as yet unnamed, was due to be ordered in 2000 for launch in November 2005; all four were scheduled to be in commission by July 2007. *Le Triomphant* began sea trials in April 1994, and her first sea cruise took place from 16 July to 22 August 1995. The first submerged launch of an M45 SLBM (range 8000km/4300nm, 6 MRVs) was made on 14 February 1995. The vessels will replace the Inflexible class.

SPECIFICATIONS

COUNTRY: France
LAUNCH DATE: 13 July 1993
CREW: 111
DISPLACEMENT: surfaced 12,842 tonnes (12640 tons); submerged 14,335 tonnes (14,565 tons)
DIMENSIONS: 138m x 17m x 12.5m (452ft 9in x 77ft 9in x 41ft)
ARMAMENT: 16 M45/TN75 SLBM; four 533mm (21in) torpedo tubes
POWERPLANT: pump jet, one nuclear PWR, two diesels
RANGE: unlimited
PERFORMANCE: surfaced 20 knots; submerged 25 knots

Los Angeles

The lead ship of this class, *Los Angeles*, was commissioned on 13 November 1976. She was followed by 52 more, the last of which, *Cheyenne*, was commissioned on 13 September 1996. They are nuclear attack submarines (SSN), fulfilling a variety of roles: land attack with onboard GDC/Hughes Tomahawk TLAM-N missiles, anti-ship with the Harpoon SSM and anti-submarine Mk48 and ADCAP (Advanced Capability) torpedoes, first fired by the USS *Norfolk* on 23 July 1988. Nine of the class were involved in the Gulf War of 1991, two firing Tomahawk missiles at targets in Iraq from stations in the eastern Mediterranean. By 1991, 75 per cent of the attack submarine force was equipped with the Tomahawk; from SN719 (USS *Providence*) onwards all are equipped with the vertical launch system, with 12 launch tubes external to the pressure hull.

SPECIFICATIONS

COUNTRY: United States
LAUNCH DATE: 06 April 1974
CREW: 133
DISPLACEMENT: surfaced 6180 tonnes (6082 tons); submerged 7038 tonnes (6927 tons)
DIMENSIONS: 110.3m x 10.1m x 9.9m (362ft x 33ft 2in x 32ft 3in)
ARMAMENT: four 533mm (21in) torpedo tubes; Tomahawk land attack cruise missiles, Harpoon SSM
POWERPLANT: single shaft, nuclear PWR, turbines
RANGE: unlimited
PERFORMANCE: surfaced 20 knots; submerged 32 knots

M4 missile

Twice the weight of the M20, the M4 can be fired more rapidly and from a greater operating depth than its predecessor. The missile entered service in 1985 aboard the *Inflexible*, France's sixth ballistic-missile submarine, allowing the French Navy to maintain three vessels on patrol at all times. The design of the missile was started in 1976 and it was fired for the first time in 1980. In its original form, the M4 had a range of 4500km (2425nm), but an improved version with a range of 5000km (2695nm) entered service in 1987 on *Le Tonnant*, when that vessel completed its retrofit. The additional range was obtained by installing the lighter TN71 nuclear warhead. An advanced version of the M4, the Aérospatiale M45/TN75, arms the submarines of Le Triomphant class. This in turn is to be replaced by the M51, with a range of 8000km (4300nm) in about 2010.

SPECIFICATIONS

COUNTRY: France
LAUNCH DATE: n/a
CREW: n/a
DISPLACEMENT: n/a
DIMENSIONS: 1.92m x 11m (6ft 3in x 36ft 3in)
ARMAMENT: n/a
POWERPLANT: n/a
RANGE: 4000km (2156nm)
PERFORMANCE: solid-propellant rocket

Marlin

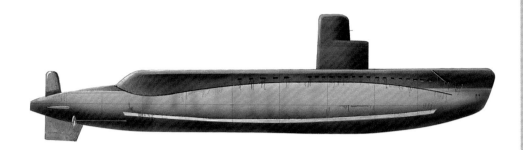

The target submarines (SSTs) *Mackerel* and *Marlin* were authorized in the Fiscal Year 1951 and 1952 shipbuilding programmes, respectively. They were the smallest American submarines built since the C class of 1909, and were intended specifically for anti-submarine training. During 1966–67, the *Mackerel* evaluated equipment for the deep submergence vehicle NR-1, including keel-mounted wheels for rolling over the ocean floor, thrusters, external television cameras, a manipulator arm, and experimental sonar. The *Mackerel* 'bottomed' 225 times during the nine-month evaluation. *Mackerel* and *Marlin* were originally designated T-1 and T-2, being named in 1956. *Mackerel* was built by the Electric Boat Company and *Marlin* by the Portsmouth Naval Yard; both were stricken in January 1973.

SPECIFICATIONS

COUNTRY: United States
LAUNCH DATE: 17 July 1953
CREW: 18
DISPLACEMENT: surfaced 308 tonnes (303 tons); submerged 353 tonnes (347 tons)
DIMENSIONS: 40m x 4.1m x 3.7m (131ft 2in x 13ft 6in x 12ft 2in)
ARMAMENT: one 533mm (21in) torpedo tube
POWERPLANT: single shaft, diesel/electric motors
RANGE: 3706km (2000nm) at 8 knots
PERFORMANCE: surfaced 8 knots; submerged 9.5 knots

Marsopa

Marsopa is one of four Daphné class boats of French design manufactured under licence in Spain, the others being *Delfin*, *Tonina* and *Narval*. All the Spanish boats underwent updates and modifications similar to those applied to the French vessels. The Daphné class, dogged by misfortune in its early operational days, went on to be an export success. In addition to the 11 French and four Spanish units, Portugal received the *Albacore*, *Barracuda*, *Cachalote* and *Delfin*, while Pakistan took delivery of the *Hangor*, *Shushuk* and *Mangro* (and also, later, Portugal's *Cachalote*, which was renamed *Ghazi*). In 1971, the *Hangor* made the first submarine attack since World War II, sinking the Indian frigate *Khukri* during the Indo-Pakistan war. South Africa also received three boats of this type.

SPECIFICATIONS

COUNTRY: Spain
LAUNCH DATE: 15 March 1974
CREW: 45
DISPLACEMENT: surfaced 884 tonnes (870 tons); submerged 1062 tonnes (1045 tons)
DIMENSIONS: 58m x 7m x 4.6m (189ft 8in x 22ft 4in x 15ft 1in)
ARMAMENT: 12 552mm (21.7in) torpedo tubes
POWERPLANT: two diesels, two electric motors
RANGE: 8338km (4300nm) at 5 knots
PERFORMANCE: surfaced 13.5 knots; submerged 16 knots

Mk 37 torpedo

The original Mk 37 Mod 0 heavyweight torpedo entered service in 1956 as a submarine- and surface ship-launched acoustic-homing free-running torpedo. As operational experience with the weapon accumulated, many Mod 0 torpedoes were refurbished to bring them up to Mk 37 Mod 3 standard. Although useful in the ASW role these free-running torpedoes, which could dive to 300m (985ft), were not suited to really long sonar detection ranges as during the weapon's run to a predicted target location it was possible that the target might perform evasive manoeuvres, taking it out of the 640m (2100ft) acquisition range of the weapon's seeker head. Therefore, successive models of the Mk 37 became wire-guided, the first entering service with the USN in 1962. The Mk 37 was withdrawn in the 1980s.

SPECIFICATIONS

COUNTRY: United States
LAUNCH DATE: n/a
CREW: n/a
DISPLACEMENT: n/a
DIMENSIONS: 484mm x 3.52m (19in x 11ft 6in)
ARMAMENT: n/a
POWERPLANT: n/a
RANGE: 18.3km (9.8nm)
PERFORMANCE: 33.6 knots

Mk 46 torpedo

Development of the lightweight Mk 46 active/passive acoustic homing torpedo began in 1960, the first rounds of the air-launched Mk 46 Mod 0 variant being delivered in 1963. The new torpedo achieved twice the range of the Mk 44, which it replaced, could dive deeper – 460m (1500ft) against 300m (984ft) – and it was 50 per cent faster (45 knots against 30). The improvement stemmed from the use of a new type of propulsion system. In the Mod 0 this was a solid-fuel motor, but as a result of maintenance difficulties it had to be changed to the Otto-fuelled thermo-chemical cam engine in the follow-on Mk 46 Mod 1, which first entered service in 1967. The latest version is the Mk 46 NEARTIP (NEAR-Term Improvement Program), designed to enhance the torpedo's capability against vessels with anechoic coatings.

SPECIFICATIONS

COUNTRY: United States
LAUNCH DATE: n/a
CREW: n/a
DISPLACEMENT: n/a
DIMENSIONS: 324mm x 2.6m (12.75in x 8ft 6in)
ARMAMENT: n/a
POWERPLANT: n/a
RANGE: 11km (6nm)
PERFORMANCE: 40/45 knots

Mk 48 torpedo

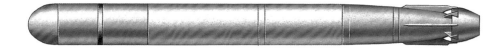

The Mk 48 heavyweight torpedo is the latest in a long line of 533mm (21in) submarine-launched weapons. As a long-range selectable-speed wire-guided dual-role weapon it replaced both the Mk 37 series and the US Navy's only nuclear-armed torpedo, the anti-ship Mk 45 ASTOR, which was fitted with a 10kT W34 warhead. Development of the Mk 48 began in 1957 when feasibility studies were initiated to meet an operational requirement eventually issued in 1960. The weapon was intended as both a surface- and a submarine-launched torpedo, but the former requirement was dropped when surface-launched weapons went out of favour. The latest variant is the Mk 48 Mod 5 ADCAP (ADvanced CAPability) torpedo, which has a higher-powered sonar to improve target acquisition and to reduce the effect of decoys and anechoic coatings.

SPECIFICATIONS

COUNTRY: United States
LAUNCH DATE: n/a
CREW: n/a
DISPLACEMENT: n/a
DIMENSIONS: 533mm x 5.8m (21in x 19ft 1in)
ARMAMENT: n/a
POWERPLANT: n/a
RANGE: 38km (23.75 miles)
PERFORMANCE: 55/60 knots

Näcken

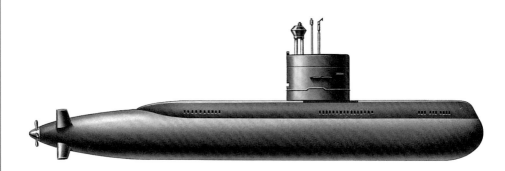

Built under a March 1973 contract by the Kockums and Karlskrona Navy Yard, the A14-type attack submarine *Näcken* and her two sisters, *Neptun* and *Najad*, are fitted with Kollmorgen periscopes. They have two decks and a 'teardrop' hull design. Their Saab NEDPS system uses two Censor 392 computers to give engine and tactical information. In 1987–88, *Näcken* was fitted with two United Stirling Type V4-275 closed-cycle engines, increasing her overall length by 8m (26ft 3in). The advantage of this powerplant is that it is independent of oxygen, so *Näcken* can remain submerged for up to 14 days. The three boats were specifically designed to counter incursions into Swedish territorial waters by Russian Whiskey-class diesel/electric boats, which continued at regular intervals during the Cold War era.

SPECIFICATIONS

COUNTRY: Sweden
LAUNCH DATE: 17 April 1978
CREW: 19
DISPLACEMENT: surfaced 996 tonnes (980 tons); submerged 1168 tonnes (1150 tons)
DIMENSIONS: 44m x 5.7m x 5.5m (144ft 4in x 18ft 8in x 18ft)
ARMAMENT: six 533mm (21in) and two 400mm (15.7in) torpedo tubes
POWERPLANT: single shaft, diesel/electric motors
RANGE: 3335km (1800nm) at 10 knots
PERFORMANCE: surfaced 20 knots; submerged 25 knots

Narwhal

The USS *Narwhal* (SSN671) was constructed in 1966–67 to evaluate the natural-circulation SSG nuclear reactor plant. This uses natural convection rather than several circulator pumps, with their associated electrical and control equipment, for heat transfer operations via the reactor coolant to the steam generators, effectively reducing at low speeds one of the major sources of self-generated machinery noise within ordinary nuclear reactor-powered submarines. In all other respects the boat was similar to the Sturgeon class SSNs. The other SSN built for powerplant research purposes was the USS *Glenard P. Lipscomb*, which evaluated a turbine-electric drive propulsion unit. Thanks to research of this kind, the American SSNs were much quieter than their Russian counterparts. Both submarines were fully operational units in the Atlantic until the late 1980s.

SPECIFICATIONS

COUNTRY: United States
LAUNCH DATE: 9 September 1967
CREW: 141
DISPLACEMENT: surfaced 4521 tonnes (4450 tons); submerged 5436 tonnes (5350 tons)
DIMENSIONS: 95.9m x 11.6m x 7.9m (314ft 8in x 38ft 1in x 25ft 11in)
ARMAMENT: four 533mm (21in) torpedo tubes; SUBROC and Sub Harpoon missiles
POWERPLANT: single shaft, nuclear PWR, turbines
RANGE: unlimited
PERFORMANCE: surfaced 18 knots; submerged 26 knots

N

Nautilus

Nautilus was the world's first nuclear-powered submarine. Apart from her revolutionary propulsion system, she was a conventional design. Early trials established new records, including nearly 2250km (1213nm) submerged in 90 hours at 20 knots, at that time the longest period spent underwater by an American submarine, as well as being the fastest speed submerged. There were two prototype nuclear attack submarines; the other, USS *Seawolf*, was launched in July 1955, the last US submarine to feature a traditional conning tower, as distinct from the fin of later nuclear submarines. *Nautilus* was the more successful; *Seawolf* was designed around the S2G reactor, intended as a backup to the S2W, but it had many operational problems and was replaced by an S2W in 1959. *Nautilus* was preserved as a museum exhibit at Groton, Connecticut, in 1982.

SPECIFICATIONS

COUNTRY: United States
LAUNCH DATE: 21 January 1954
CREW: 105
DISPLACEMENT: surfaced 4157 tonnes (4091 tons); submerged 4104 tonnes (4040 tons)
DIMENSIONS: 97m x 8.4m x 6.6m (323ft 7in x 27ft 8in x 21ft 9in)
ARMAMENT: six 533mm (21in) torpedo tubes
POWERPLANT: twin screws, one S2W reactor, turbines
RANGE: unlimited
PERFORMANCE: surfaced 20 knots; submerged 23 knots

Nazario Sauro

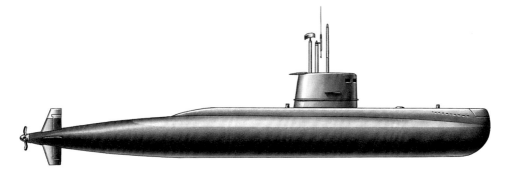

During the early 1970s, it became apparent to the Supermarina (Italian Admiralty) that a new submarine design was required for defence against amphibious landings and for ASW and anti-shipping tasks in the local area. The result was the Sauro class. The first two units were the *Nazario Sauro* and *Carlo Fecia de Cossato*, which entered service in 1980 and 1979 respectively, following a delay caused by major problems with their batteries. A further two units, the *Leonardo da Vinci* and *Guglielmo Marconi*, were then ordered and these were commissioned into service in 1981 and 1982. They were to have been followed in 1987–88 by the last pair, *Salvatore Pelosi* and *Giuliano Prini*, but these were cancelled. If required, the submarines' torpedo armament can be replaced by several varieties of Italian-made ground mine.

SPECIFICATIONS

COUNTRY: Italy
LAUNCH DATE: 9 October 1976
CREW: 45
DISPLACEMENT: surfaced 1479 tonnes (1456 tons); submerged 1657 tonnes (1631 tons)
DIMENSIONS: 63.9m x 6.8m x 5.7m (209ft 7in x 22ft 4in x 18ft 8in)
ARMAMENT: six 533mm (21in) torpedo tubes
POWERPLANT: single shaft, diesel/electric motors
RANGE: 12,971km (7000nm) at 10 knots
PERFORMANCE: surfaced 11 knots; submerged 20 knots

November class

Built as Russia's first nuclear submarine design from 1958 to 1963 at Severodvinsk, the November-class SSN was designed for the anti-ship rather than the anti-submarine role. They carried a full load of 24 nuclear torpedoes. They were provided with a targeting radar for use with the strategic-attack torpedo, presmably to confirm its position off an enemy coast. Thus armed, the task of these boats was to attack carrier battle groups. They were very noisy underwater and were prone to reactor leaks, which did not endear them to their crews. In April 1970, a November-class boat was lost southwest of the United Kingdom after an internal fire, the surviving crew being taken off before the boat sank, and there were numerous other incidents involving the boats during their operational career. All 14 boats were retired in the 1980s.

SPECIFICATIONS

COUNTRY: Russia
LAUNCH DATE: 1958
CREW: 86
DISPLACEMENT: surfaced 4267 tonnes (4200 tons); submerged 5080 tonnes (5000 tons)
DIMENSIONS: 109.7m x 9.1m x 6.7m (359ft 11in x 29ft 10in x 22ft)
ARMAMENT: eight 533mm (21in) and two 406mm (16in) torpedo tubes
POWERPLANT: twin shafts, one nuclear PWR, two turbines
RANGE: unlimited
PERFORMANCE: surfaced 20 knots; submerged 30 knots

Oberon

Built between 1959 and 1967 as a follow-on to the Porpoise class, the Oberon class was outwardly identical to its predecessor, although there were internal differences. These included the soundproofing of all equipment for silent running and the use of a high-grade steel for the hull to allow a greater maximum diving depth of up to 340m (1115ft). A total of 13 units was commissioned into the Royal Navy. *Oberon* was modified with a deeper casing to house equipment for the initial training of personnel for the nuclear submarine fleet but was paid off for disposal in 1986, together with HMS *Orpheus*. One of the class, *Onyx*, served in the South Atlantic during the Falklands war on periscope beach reconnaissance operations and for landing special forces. During these operations she rammed a rock, causing one of her torpedoes to become stuck in its tube.

SPECIFICATIONS

COUNTRY: United Kingdom
LAUNCH DATE: 18 July 1959
CREW: 69
DISPLACEMENT: surfaced 2063 tonnes (2030 tons); submerged 2449 tonnes (2410 tons)
DIMENSIONS: 90m x 8.1m x 5.5m (295ft 3in x 26ft 6in x 18ft 1in)
ARMAMENT: eight 533mm (21in) torpedo tubes
POWERPLANT: two shafts, two diesel/electric motors
RANGE: 11,118km (6000nm) at 10 knots
PERFORMANCE: surfaced 12 knots; submerged 17.5 knots

O

Oscar class

The underwater equivalent of a Kirov-class battlecruiser, the first Oscar I-class cruise-missile submarine (SSGN) was laid down at Severodvinsk in 1978 and launched in the spring of 1980, starting sea trials later that year. The second was completed in 1982, and a third of the class – which became the first Oscar II – completed in 1985, followed by a fourth, fifth and sixth at intervals of a year. The primary task of the Oscar class was to attack NATO carrier battle groups with a variety of submarine-launched cruise missiles, including the SS-N-19 Shipwreck; this has a range of 445km (240nm) at Mach 1.6. The SSM tubes are in banks of 12 either side and external to the pressure hull and are inclined at 40°, with one hatch covering each pair. Two Oscar Is and eight Oscar IIs were in service by 1990.

SPECIFICATIONS

COUNTRY: Russia
LAUNCH DATE: April 1980
CREW: 130
DISPLACEMENT: surfaced 11,685 tonnes (11,500 tons); submerged 13,615 tonnes (13,400 tons)
DIMENSIONS: 143m x 18.2m x 9m (469ft 2in x 59ft 8in x 29ft 6in)
ARMAMENT: SS-N-15, SS-N-16 and SS-N-19 SSMs; four 533mm (21in) and four 650mm (25.6in) torpedo tubes
POWERPLANT: two shafts; two nuclear PWR; two turbines
RANGE: unlimited
PERFORMANCE: surfaced 22 knots; submerged 30 knots

Oyashio

The first two boats in a new class of Japanese SSK, *Oyashio* and *Michishio*, were laid down in January 1994 and February 1995 respectively. Five boats are planned in all, the construction work shared between Mitsubishi and Kawasaki at the Kobe shipyards. Although some damage was caused to the latter by the Kobe earthquake in January 1995, production was not disrupted. The boats are fitted with large flank sonar arrays; there are anechoic tiles on the fin and double hull sections fore and aft. The class was developed from the earlier Harushio-class boats and the two classes strongly resemble one another, although the Oyashios have a greater displacement. The fifth boat is due to commission on March 2002. The Oyashios are thought to have a greater endurance than any previous Japanese submarines.

SPECIFICATIONS

COUNTRY: Japan
LAUNCH DATE: 15 October 1996
CREW: 69
DISPLACEMENT: surfaced 2743 tonnes (2700 tons); submerged 3048 tonnes (3000 tons)
DIMENSIONS: 81.7m x 8.9m x 7.9m (268ft x 29ft 2in x 25ft 11in)
ARMAMENT: six 533mm (21in) torpedo tubes; sub harpoon SSM
POWERPLANT: single shaft, diesel/electric motors
RANGE: classified
PERFORMANCE: surfaced 12 knots; submerged 20 knots

Papa

In 1970, the Soviet shipyard at Severodvinsk launched a single unit of what came to be known in NATO circles as the Papa class. The boat was considerably larger and had two more missile tubes than the contemporary Charlie-class SSGNs, and was a puzzle to Western intelligence services. The answer appeared in 1980 at the same shipyard with the even larger Oscar-class SSGN; the Papa-class unit had been the prototype for advanced SSGN concepts with a considerably changed powerplant and a revised screw arrangement incorporating five or seven blades. The missile system's function had been to test the underwater-launched version of the SS-N-9 Siren for the subsequent Charlie II series of SSGN. The Oscar design produced yet further improvements, with two 12-round banks of submerged-launch long-range SS-N19 anti-ship missile tubes.

SPECIFICATIONS

COUNTRY: Russia
LAUNCH DATE: 1970
CREW: 110
DISPLACEMENT: surfaced 6198 tonnes (6100 tons); submerged 7112 tonnes (7000 tons)
DIMENSIONS: 109m x 11.5m x 7.6m (357ft 7in x 37ft 9in x 24ft 11in)
ARMAMENT: six 533mm (21in) and two 406mm (16in) torpedo tubes
POWERPLANT: two shafts, one nuclear PWR, two turbines
RANGE: unlimited
PERFORMANCE: surfaced 20 knots; submerged 39 knots

Pickerel

The Tench class marked the ultimate refinement in the basic design whose ancestry could be traced back to the P class. Externally they were virtually identical to the Balao class. Only a dozen managed to see operational duty in World War II and none of these was lost. Total production was 33 boats between 1944 and 1946, with another 101 cancelled or scrapped incomplete. Differences from the earlier Balaos, though not obvious, were significant. Engine noise was reduced, and the fuel and ballast tanks were better organized. Even a further four torpedo reloads were squeezed in, and this, combined with radar and efficient mechanical fire-control computers put the Tenches way ahead of the opposition. *Pickerel* was transferred to Italy in 1972 after extensive updating, where she served under the name *Gianfranco Gazzana Priaroggia* until 1981.

SPECIFICATIONS

COUNTRY: United States
LAUNCH DATE: 15 December 1944
CREW: 22
DISPLACEMENT: surfaced 1595 tonnes (1570 tons); submerged 2453 tonnes (2415 tons)
DIMENSIONS: 95.2m x 8.31m x 4.65m (311ft 8in x 27ft 3in x 15ft 3in)
ARMAMENT: one or two 127mm (5in) guns; 10 533mmTT for 28 torpedoes
POWERPLANT: four diesels and two electric motors
RANGE: 20,372km (11,000nm) at 10 knots
PERFORMANCE: surfaced 20.2 knots; submerged 8.7 knots

Piper

Piper (SS409) was a double-hull, ocean-going submarine with good seakeeping qualities and range. She was one of the Gato class of over 300 boats, and as such was part of the largest warship project undertaken by the US Navy. These boats were to wreak havoc on Japan's mercantile shipping in the Pacific war. *Piper* was originally named *Awa* and, like many other Gato-class boats, was built at the Portsmouth Naval Dockyard. She deployed to the Pacific late in 1944, and became combat-ready early in the New Year. On 10 February 1945, together with the submarines *Sterlet*, *Pomfret*, *Trepang*, *Bowfin*, *Sennet*, *Lagarto* and *Haddock*, she hunted enemy patrol boats that might have detected the presence of Vice-Admiral Mitscher's Task Force 58, which was heading for Iwo Jima. *Piper* was placed in reserve some years after the war and was stricken in 1970.

SPECIFICATIONS

COUNTRY: United States
LAUNCH DATE: 26 June 1944
CREW: 80
DISPLACEMENT: surfaced 1854 tonnes (1825 tons); submerged 2448 tonnes (2410 tons)
DIMENSIONS: 95m x 8.3m x 4.6m (311ft 9in x 27ft 3in x 15ft 3in)
ARMAMENT: ten 533mm (21in) torpedo tubes; one 76mm (3in) gun
POWERPLANT: twin screw diesels, electric motors
RANGE: 22,236km (12,000nm) at 10 knots
PERFORMANCE: surfaced 20 knots; submerged 10 knots

Polaris A3

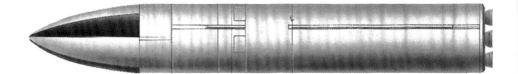

The last user of the Polaris SLBM was the Royal Navy, which had its stock of missiles re-engined in the mid-1980s so that it could provide a viable strategic missile force until the deployment of Trident. The British missiles (133 in all) were armed with three British-designed MIRVs for use against area targets such as cities and oilfields. The effect of a single high-yield warhead falls off rapidly with distance from the point of impact, whereas several lower-yield warheads around the target perimeter cause significantly more damage. The UK Polaris missiles were hardened and equipped with penetration aids as a result of a project called Chevaline, which resulted in the weapon being redesignated Polaris A3TK. The Chevaline project was prompted by Soviet developments in ABM defences.

SPECIFICATIONS

COUNTRY: United States
LAUNCH DATE: n/a
CREW: n/a
DISPLACEMENT: n/a
DIMENSIONS: 1.4m x 9.8m (4ft 6in x 32ft 2in)
ARMAMENT: n/a
POWERPLANT: n/a
RANGE: 4748km (2559nm)
PERFORMANCE: not known

Poseidon C3

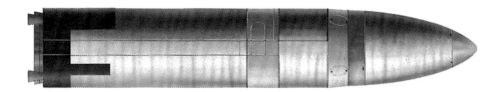

By 1964, two follow-on designs to the Polaris were under review. One subsequently evolved into the Lockheed UGM-73A Poseidon SLBM, which could use the launch tubes of exisitng SSBNs. Ultimately, 31 out of the 41 SSBNs built were refitted to carry Poseidon, although some were later fitted to carry Trident I. The Poseidon C3 entered operational service in 1970. The missile introduced the concept of multiple warheads to American SLBMs, and penetration aids were also fitted. The two-stage solid-propellant missiles were targeted mainly against soft military and industrial objectives such as airfields, storage depots and above-ground command and control facilities. One problem for an SSBN commander is that he would prefer all his SLBMs to be launched in one go, not in several groups, because each firing points to his location.

SPECIFICATIONS

COUNTRY: United States
LAUNCH DATE: n/a
CREW: n/a
DISPLACEMENT: n/a
DIMENSIONS: 1.9m x 10.4m (6ft 2in x 34ft)
ARMAMENT: n/a
POWERPLANT: n/a
RANGE: 4000–5200km (2156–2803nm) depending on warheads carried
PERFORMANCE: not known

Redoutable

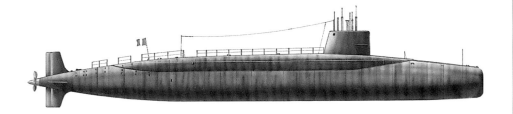

L aid down at Cherbourg Naval Dockyard on 30 March 1964, the *Redoutable* was France's first ballistic-missile submarine, and the prototype of the seaborne element of the French Force de Dissuasion (Deterrent Force), which ultimately consisted of boats armed with the MSBS (Mer-Sol Ballistique Strategique) IRBM. The French term for SSBN is SNLE (Sous-marin Nucleaire Lance-Engins). The *Redoutable* reached IOC in December 1971; *Le Terrible* followed in 1973, *Le Foudroyant* in 1974, *Indomptable* in 1977 and *Le Tonnant* in 1979. Later, all units except the *Redoutable* were armed with the Aerospatiale M4 three-stage solid fuel missile, which has a range of 5300km (2860nm) and carries six MIRV, each of 150kT. The M4 missiles can be discharged at twice the rate of the M20. The *Redoutable* was withdrawn in 1991.

SPECIFICATIONS

COUNTRY: France
LAUNCH DATE: 29 March 1967
CREW: 142
DISPLACEMENT: surfaced 7620 tonnes (7500 tons); submerged 9144 tons (9000 tons)
DIMENSIONS: 128m x 10.6m x 10m (420ft x 34ft 10in x 32ft 10in)
ARMAMENT: 16 submarine-launched MRBMs
POWERPLANT: one nuclear PWR, turbines
RANGE: unlimited
PERFORMANCE: surfaced 20 knots; submerged 28 knots

Requin

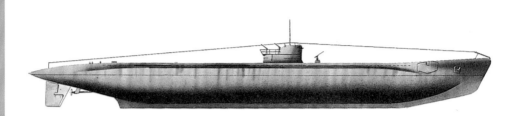

Remo was leader of the R class of 12 transport submarines, the largest Italian boats built up to that time. Laid down in September 1942, she was completed in June 1943. She had four watertight holds with a total capacity of 600m² (21,190ft²). Maximum diving depth was 100m (328ft). She and her one operational sister, *Romolo*, were developed to transport cargo to and from the Far East. Ten more vessels in the class were laid down; two (*R3* and *R4*) were launched in 1946 and then scrapped, two (*R5* and *R6*) were scrapped on the slip, and the rest were either scuttled or sunk in air attacks after being seized by German forces. *R11* and *R12* were subsequently refloated and used as oil storage vessels for some years after the war. *Remo* was sunk by HMS *United* on her maiden voyage in the Gulf of Taranto on 15 July 1943.

SPECIFICATIONS

COUNTRY: Italy
LAUNCH DATE: 28 March 1943
CREW: 63
DISPLACEMENT: surfaced 2245 tonnes (2210 tons); submerged 2648 tonnes (2606 tons)
DIMENSIONS: 70.7m x 7.8m x 5.3m (232ft x 25ft 9in x 17ft 6in)
ARMAMENT: three 20mm (0.8in) guns
POWERPLANT: twin screws, diesel/electric motors
RANGE: 22,236km (12,000nm) at 9 knots
PERFORMANCE: surfaced 13 knots; submerged 6 knots

Remo

Requin is one of six Narval-class diesel-electric boats laid down for the French Navy between 1951 and 1956. The requirement was for a submarine of 1219 tonnes (1200 tons) standard displacement, with a surfaced speed of 16 knots and a range of 27,795km (15,000nm) with snorkel. France still had substantial colonial interests in the Pacific and Indo-China, making it imperative for the new class of submarine to be capable of a fast transit over long distances followed by a patrol of seven to fourteen days. The Narvals were in fact improved versions of the German Type XXI, one of which had been extensively tested after the war under the name Roland Morillot. The other boats in the class were *Dauphin* (Dolphin), *Espadon* (Swordfish), *Marsouin* (*Porpoise*), *Morse* (Walrus) and *Narval* (Narwhal) – names taken from a pre-war class of French submarine.

SPECIFICATIONS

COUNTRY: France
LAUNCH DATE: 3 December 1955
CREW: 63
DISPLACEMENT: surfaced 1661 tonnes (1635 tons); submerged 1941 tonnes (1910 tons)
DIMENSIONS: 78.4m x 7.8m x 5.2m (257ft 3in x 25ft 7in x 17ft 1in)
ARMAMENT: eight 550mm (21.7in) torpedo tubes
POWERPLANT: two shafts, diesel/electric motors
RANGE: 27,795km (15,000nm) at 8 knots
PERFORMANCE: surfaced 16 knots; submerged 18 knots

RO-100

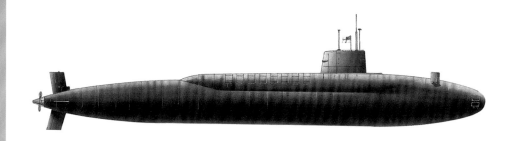

In February 1963, the British Government stated its intention to order four or five Resolution-class nuclear-powered ballistic missile submarines, armed with the American Polaris SLBM, to take over the British nuclear deterrent role from the RAF from 1968. With characteristics very similar to the American Lafayettes, the lead ship HMS *Resolution* was commissioned in October 1967. HMS *Repulse* followed in September 1968, with the HMS *Renown* and HMS *Revenge* commissioning in November 1968 and December 1969 respectively. Early in 1968, *Resolution* undertook missile trials with Polaris off Florida, and four months later she made her first operational patrol. In the 1990s the Resolution-class boats were progressively replaced by the new Vanguard class SSBNs, armed with the Trident II missile. The first of these was commissioned in August 1993.

SPECIFICATIONS

COUNTRY: United Kingdom
LAUNCH DATE: September 1966
CREW: 154
DISPLACEMENT: surfaced 7620 tonnes (7500 tons); submerged 8535 tonnes (8400 tons)
DIMENSIONS: 129.5m x 10.1m x 9.1m (425ft x 33ft 2in x 29ft 10in)
ARMAMENT: 16 Polaris A3TK IRBMs; six 533mm (21in) torpedo tubes
POWERPLANT: single shaft, one nuclear PWR, two steam turbines
RANGE: unlimited
PERFORMANCE: surfaced 20 knots; submerged 25 knots

Resolution

Ordered under the Japanese Navy's 1940 and 1941 programmes, the RO-100 (Type KS) class were designed as coastal submarines to be used around the Japanese coastline and in the waters of the outposts of the Japanese Empire. Designed to operate near their bases, their operational endurance was only 21 days. Submerged range was 111km (60nm) at 3 knots, and they had a diving depth of 75m (245ft). Production was shared between the Kure Navy Yard and the Kawasaki Yard at Kobe. None of the class survived the war, during which they sank six merchant ships totalling 35,247 tonnes (34,690 tons) and damaged three more, totalling 14,300 tonnes (14,074 tons). In addition, *RO-106* (under Lt Nakamura) sank the tank landing ship *LST 342* off New Georgia on 18 July 1943, while *RO-108* sank the US destroyer *Henley* off Finschhafen (New Guinea) on 3 October 1943.

SPECIFICATIONS

COUNTRY: Japan
LAUNCH DATE: 1942
CREW: 75
DISPLACEMENT: surfaced 611 tonnes (601 tons); submerged 795 tonnes (782 tons)
DIMENSIONS: 57.4m x 6.1m x 3.5m (188ft 3in x 20ft x 11ft 6in)
ARMAMENT: four 533mm (21in) torpedo tubes; one 76mm (3in) gun
POWERPLANT: two shaft diesels plus electric motors
RANGE: 6485km (3500nm) at 12 knots
PERFORMANCE: surfaced 14 knots; submerged 8 knots

Romeo

Roland Morillot was the former German Type XXI U-boat U2518, one of a group of Horten-based submarines that surrendered to the British in May 1945. She was transferred to France in 1946, and renamed in the following year. The Type XXI was an ocean-going submarine capable of fully-submerged operations with the use of Snorkel apparatus. A conventional diesel-electric boat, it had a streamlined hull of all-welded construction which, in order to speed production, was prefabricated in eight sections. The Type XXI was equipped with chin sonar; it could carry a very useful load of 23 torpedoes, or 12 torpedoes plus 12 mines. France tested the vessel exhaustively, and the lessons learned were incorporated in the Requin-class submarines of the 1950s. Roland Morillot was stricken from the French navy list in 1968.

SPECIFICATIONS

COUNTRY: France
LAUNCH DATE: 1944
CREW: 57
DISPLACEMENT: surfaced 1638 tonnes (1612 tons); submerged 1848 tonnes (1819 tons)
DIMENSIONS: 76.5m x 7m x 6m (251ft x 23ft x 19ft 8in)
ARMAMENT: six 533mm (21in) torpedo tubes
POWERPLANT: single shaft, diesel/electric motors
RANGE: 17,933km (9678nm) at 12 knots
PERFORMANCE: surfaced 15.5 knots; submerged 16 knots

Roland Morillot

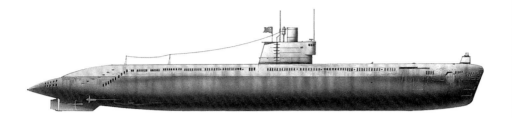

Although it was the Russians who built the first Romeo-class submarines in 1958 at Gorky as an improvement on the Whiskey design, their construction coincided with the successful introduction of nuclear propulsion into Soviet submarines, so only 20 were completed out of the 560 boats originally planned. The design was passed to the Chinese and production began in China in 1962, at the Jiangnan (Shanghai) shipyard under the local designation Type 003. Three further shipyards then joined to give a maximum yearly production rate of nine units during the early 1970s. Production was completed in 1984 with a total of 98 built for the Chinese Navy; four more were exported to Egypt and seven to North Korea, with a further ten built locally with Chinese assistance. In February 1985, the North Koreans lost one of their Romeos with all hands in the Yellow Sea.

SPECIFICATIONS

COUNTRY: China
LAUNCH DATE: 1962
CREW: 60
DISPLACEMENT: surfaced 1351 tonnes (1330 tons); submerged 1727 tonnes (1700 tons)
DIMENSIONS: 77m x 6.7m x 4.9m (252ft 7in x 22ft x 16ft 1in)
ARMAMENT: eight 533mm (21in) torpedo tubes
POWERPLANT: twin screws, diesel/electric motors
RANGE: 29,632km (16,000nm) at 10 knots
PERFORMANCE: surfaced 16 knots; submerged 13 knots

Rubis

The Saphir class of Fleet Nuclear-Attack Submarines (Sous-Marins Nucléaires d'Attaque, or SNA) comprises eight vessels, in two squadrons, one based at Lorient to cover the SSBN base and the other at Toulon. Eight boats are in service; *Rubis* (S601), *Saphir* (S602), *Casabianca* (S603), *Emeraude* (S604), *Améthyste* (S605), *Perle* (S606), *Turquoise* (S607) and *Diamant* (S608). The last five were built to a modified design, including a new bow form and silencing system, as well as new tactical and attack systems and improved electronics. The boats have a diving depth of 300m (984ft). Apart from the experimental 406-tonne (400-ton) NR-1 of the US Navy, *Saphir* is the smallest nuclear-attack submarine ever built, reflecting France's advanced nuclear-reactor technology. *Rubis* became operational in February 1983; the last, *Diamant*, in 1999.

SPECIFICATIONS

COUNTRY: France
LAUNCH DATE: 7 July 1979
CREW: 67
DISPLACEMENT: surfaced 2423 tonnes (2385 tons); submerged 2713 tonnes (2670 tons)
DIMENSIONS: 72.1m x 7.6m x 6.4m (236ft 6in x 24ft 11in x 21ft)
ARMAMENT: four 533mm (21in) torpedo tubes; Exocet SSMs
POWERPLANT: single shaft, one nuclear PWR, auxiliary diesel/electric
RANGE: unlimited
PERFORMANCE: surfaced 25 knots; submerged classified

San Francisco

Originally designed as a counter to the Russian Victor-class SSN, *San Francisco* is one of a class of versatile vessels, fulfilling a variety of roles from land attack with their onboard GDC/ Hughes Tomahawk TLAM-N missiles, to anti-ship with the Harpoon SSM, and anti-submarine with their Mk48 and ADCAP (Advanced Capability) torpedoes, the first of which was fired by the USS *Norfolk* on 23 July 1988 at the target destroyer *Jonas K. Ingram*. Nine of the class were involved in the Gulf War of 1991, two firing Tomahawk missiles at targets in Iraq from stations in the eastern Mediterranean. By 1991, 75 per cent of the attack-submarine force was equipped with the Tomahawk; from SN719 (USS *Providence*) onwards all are equipped with the vertical launch system, which places 12 launch tubes external to the pressure hull behind the BQQ5 spherical array forward.

SPECIFICATIONS

COUNTRY: United States
LAUNCH DATE: 27 October 1979
CREW: 133
DISPLACEMENT: surfaced 6180 tonnes (6082 tons); submerged 7038 tonnes (6927 tons)
DIMENSIONS: 110.3m x 10.1m x 9.9m (362ft x 33ft 2in x 32ft 3in)
ARMAMENT: four 533mm (21in) torpedo tubes; Tomahawk land attack cruise missiles, Harpoon SSM
POWERPLANT: single shaft, nuclear PWR, turbines
RANGE: unlimited
PERFORMANCE: surfaced 20 knots; submerged 32 knots

Sanguine

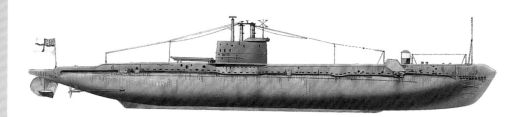

Sanguine was one of the last batch of S-class boats built by Cammell Laird and laid down in 1944–45. The class was not scheduled for any major modification post-war, but several vessels were modified for trials work. Israel bought two – *Sanguine* and *Springer* – in 1958, and named them *Rahav* and *Tanin* respectively. The latter was discarded as worn out in 1968 and cannibalized to keep *Rahav* in commission for some time longer in the training role. They were replaced in Israeli service by HMS *Turpin* and *Truncheon*, which were commissioned into the Israeli Navy as *Leviathan* and *Dolphin*. Three S-class boats: *Spur*, *Saga* and *Spearhead* were transferred to Portugal in 1948–49, while the quartet of *Styr*, *Spiteful*, *Sportsman* and *Statesman* were transferred to France in 1951–52.

SPECIFICATIONS

COUNTRY: United Kingdom
LAUNCH DATE: 15 February 1945
CREW: 44
DISPLACEMENT: surfaced 726 tonnes (715 tons); submerged 1006 tonnes (990 tons)
DIMENSIONS: 61.8m x 7.25m x 3.2m (202ft 6in x 23ft 9in x 10ft 6in)
ARMAMENT: six 533mm (21in) torpedo tubes; one 76mm (3in) gun
POWERPLANT: twin screws, diesel/electric motors
RANGE: 15,750km (8500nm) at 10 knots
PERFORMANCE: surfaced 14.7 knots; submerged 9 knots

Santa Cruz

The long-range HY80 steel-hulled Santa Cruz or TR1700 class of SSK was designed by the German firm of Thyssen Nordseewerk to meet Argentine Navy requirements. Ordered in 1977, the first two units, *Santa Cruz* and *San Juan*, were built at Emden and commissioned into the Argentine Navy in 1984 and 1985 respectively. The contract specified that four more boats were to be built in Argentina with German assistance; two, S43 (*Santiago del Esturo*) and S44 were laid down, but were still only partially completed in the mid-1990s and will probably be scrapped, their equipment, together with that of the fifth and sixth projected boats, being used for spares. *Santa Cruz* and *San Juan* were both operational in 1999 and based at Mar del Plata. The TR1700-type boats have proved to be a major export success.

SPECIFICATIONS

COUNTRY: Argentina
LAUNCH DATE: 28 September 1982
CREW: 29
DISPLACEMENT: surfaced 2150 tonnes (2116 tons); submerged 2300 tonnes (2264 tons)
DIMENSIONS: 66m x 7.3m x 6.5m (216ft 6in x 23ft 11in x 21ft 3in)
ARMAMENT: six 533mm (21in) torpedo tubes
POWERPLANT: single shaft, diesel/electric motors
RANGE: 22,224km (12,000nm) at 8 knots
PERFORMANCE: surfaced 15 knots; submerged 25 knots

Scorpène

The Scorpène's basic form is the CM-2000, but also on offer are the AM-2000, with the French MESMA system of air-independent propulsion; the CA-2000, a smaller version for coastal work; and the S-BR, a larger version supplied to the Brazilian Navy. The Spanish Government ordered four in 2003, then subsequently cancelled the order in favour of the similar S-80 Spanish-designed submarine, also built by Navantia with the Lockheed-Martin Corporation. Meanwhile, two Scorpènes have been built for Chile, commissioned in 2005 and 2006, two for Malaysia, commissioned in 2009 and three are under construction for India, with others under negotiation or construction. The Scorpène hull can carry 18 heavyweight torpedoes or missiles, or 30 mines. It can fire the latest wire-guided torpedo types and can be adapted as an anti-ship, anti-submarine or dual-purpose attack boat.

SPECIFICATIONS

COUNTRY: France
LAUNCH DATE: 2005
CREW: 31
DISPLACEMENT: submerged 1870 tonnes (1840.4 tons)
DIMENSIONS: 70m x 6.2m x 5.8m (230ft x 20ft 3in x 19ft)
ARMAMENT: six 533mm (21in) launch tubes for torpedoes/SM39 Exocet, or 30 mines
POWERPLANT: diesel-electric motors; battery/AIP
RANGE: 12,000km (6500nm) at 8kt
PERFORMANCE: surfaced 12 knots; submerged 20 knots

Seawolf

USS *Seawolf*, lead ship of her class, was conceived during the Cold War as an extremely potent attack submarine to replace the Los Angeles class. A changing naval warfare environment led to the curtailment of the class after three units, in favour of Virginia class. *Seawolf* is capable of operating under ice and is both quieter and more manoeuvrable than the Los Angeles class. She is capable of 35 knots submerged and can make 20 knots even in 'silent' mode. *Seawolf* can launch missiles and torpedoes against surface targets, and is capable of attacking deep-diving submarines. Land attack capability is provided by Tomahawk cruise missiles; a version is also available for long-range anti-ship strikes. The Seawolf class was designed with upgrade capability in mind. Members of the class are being upgraded with improved sonar processing equipment and at least one vessel is receiving major modifications.

SPECIFICATIONS

COUNTRY: United States
LAUNCH DATE: 24 June 1995
CREW: 115
DISPLACEMENT: surfaced 7568 tonnes (7448 tons); submerged 9142 tonnes (8998 tons)
DIMENSIONS: 107.6m x 12.9m x 10.9m (353ft x 42.3ft x 35ft)
ARMAMENT: eight 66m tubes capable of launching Harpoon and Tomahawk missiles or Mk 46 torpedoes. Total of 50 weapons
POWERPLANT: one GE PWR S6W nuclear reactor (56,000hp/38.8MW); one Westinghouse secondary propulsion reactor
RANGE: effectively unlimited
PERFORMANCE: surfaced 18 knots; submerged 35 knots (20 knots 'silent')

Sentinel

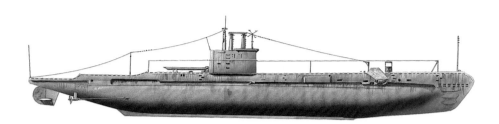

Sentinel, like *Sanguine*, was one of the later S-class boats. Built by Scotts, she was launched on 27 July 1945 and was consequently too late to be operational in World War II. A very successful submarine design, the S class had an operational diving depth of 91.5m (300ft) against the 106.75m (350ft) of the rest, which had welded pressure hull plating. *Sturdy*, *Stygian* and *Subtle* had an extra external torpedo tube at the stern and could carry 13 torpedoes; all could carry 12 M2 mines as an alternative load. A 20mm (0.79in) gun was fitted at a later date. *Selene*, *Solent* and *Sleuth* were subsequently converted as high speed target-vessels. *Sidon* was damaged by an internal explosion on 16 June 1955; the official explanation was that the blast had been caused by a gas bottle, but the real cause was concentrated hydrogen peroxide, used in experimental torpedoes.

SPECIFICATIONS

COUNTRY: United Kingdom
LAUNCH DATE: 27 July 1945
CREW: 44
DISPLACEMENT: surfaced 726 tonnes (715 tons); submerged 1006 tonnes (990 tons)
DIMENSIONS: 61.8m x 7.25m x 3.2m (202ft 6in x 23ft 9in x 10ft 6in)
ARMAMENT: six 533mm (21in) torpedo tubes; one 76mm (3in) gun
POWERPLANT: twin screws, diesel/electric motors
RANGE: 15,750km (8500nm) at 10 knots
PERFORMANCE: surfaced 14.7 knots; submerged 9 knots

Seraph

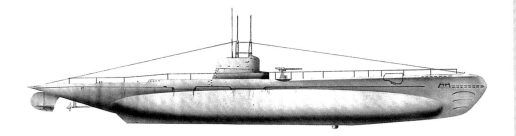

Seraph was a beacon submarine for the Allied invasion force approaching Sicily in July 1943. The expected massive submarine assault on the invasion force never materialized, although the Italian *Dandolo* succeeded in torpedoing the cruiser *Cleopatra* on 16 July. As the operation proceeded, the enemy suffered heavy submarine losses; six Italian boats were sunk, along with the German *U375*, *U409* and *U561*. The Italian submarine *Bronzo* was depth-charged to the surface on 12 July and captured intact. On 23 July, the cruiser *Newfoundland* was damaged in a torpedo attack by the *U407*, but, between D-Day and the end of July, the enemy submarines sank only four British merchantmen – one of which was torpedoed in Syracuse harbour by the *U81* – and two American LSTs. HMS *Seraph* was scrapped in December 1965.

SPECIFICATIONS

COUNTRY: United Kingdom
LAUNCH DATE: 25 October 1941
CREW: 44
DISPLACEMENT: surfaced 886 tonnes (872 tons); submerged 1005 tonnes (990 tons)
DIMENSIONS: 66.1m x 7.2m x 3.4m (216ft 10in x 23ft 8in x 11ft 2in)
ARMAMENT: six 533mm (21in) torpedo tubes; one 76mm (3in) gun
POWERPLANT: twin screws, diesel/electric motors
RANGE: 11,400km (6144nm) at 10 knots
PERFORMANCE: surfaced 14.7 knots; submerged 9 knots

Severodvinsk (Graney Class)

Severodvinsk is the lead boat of the Graney class (also known as Yasen class, or Project 885) which is a follow-on from the Akula class of nuclear powered attack submarines. It is intended that this class will replace both the Akula and Oscar class submarines currently in service. However, construction of the lead boat was delayed by funding shortages. The Graney class is armed with eight 533mm (21in) torpedo tubes which can launch anti-ship and anti-submarine torpedoes, anti-submarine rockets, mines and the supercavitating VA-111 Shkval torpedo. Shkval torpedoes have a speed of over 200knots and a range of 7,000–13,000m (22,966ft–46,650ft). There are also eight vertical launch tubes for cruise missiles with a range of 300–800km (186–497 miles). The Graney class is a multimission boat capable of supporting special forces and gathering intelligence as well as conventional anti-shipping and anti-submarine missions.

SPECIFICATIONS

COUNTRY: Russia
LAUNCH DATE: 2010
CREW: 50
DISPLACEMENT: surfaced 5800–7700 tonnes (5708–7578 tons); submerged 8200–13,000 tonnes (8070–12,795 tons)
DIMENSIONS: 111m x 12m x 8.4m (364ft 2in x 39ft 4in x 27ft 6in)
ARMAMENT: eight 533mm (21in) torpedo tubes capable of launching VA-111 Shkval torpedoes, SAET-60M, Type 65–76, Type 65K torpedoes and RPK-7/SS-N-16
POWERPLANT: pressurised water reactor
RANGE: effectively unlimited
PERFORMANCE: surfaced 20 knots; submerged 35 knots

Shark

The USS *Shark* (SSN 591) was one of the five Skipjack class SSNs built in the late 1950s. Until the advent of the Los Angeles class, they were the fastest submarines available to the US Navy, and a principal factor in the potentially deadly game of cat and mouse played by NATO and Warsaw Pact submariners for nearly three decades. The development of nuclear-attack submarines in the United States and Soviet Union began at about the same time, but the designs followed different paths. The Americans concentrating on anti-submarine warfare (ASW) and the Russians on a multi-mission role, encompassing both ASW and surface attack with large anti-ship cruise missiles. Later on, the Americans also adopted a multi-mission capability with the deployment of submarine-launched weapons like Sub-Harpoon and Tomahawk, designed for anti-ship and land attack.

SPECIFICATIONS

COUNTRY: United States
LAUNCH DATE: 16 March 1960
CREW: 106–114
DISPLACEMENT: surfaced 3124 tonnes (3075 tons); submerged 3556 tonnes (3500 tons)
DIMENSIONS: 76.7m x 9.6m x 8.5m (251ft 9in x 31ft 6in x 27ft 10in)
ARMAMENT: six 533mm (21in) torpedo tubes
POWERPLANT: single shaft, one nuclear PWR, two steam turbines
RANGE: unlimited
PERFORMANCE: surfaced 18 knots; submerged 30 knots

Sierra class

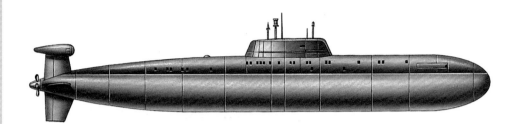

Two SSNs of the Sierra I class were laid down at Gorky and Severodvinsk shipyards in 1983, launched in July 1986 and commissioned in September 1937. The first boat, *Tula* (formerly *Karp*) was still operational in the late 1990s, but her sister vessel was deleted in 1997. *Tula* is based with the Northern Fleet at Ara Guba. *Sierra I* – known to the Russians as *Barracuda* – was augmented by two vessels of the Sierra II class, *Pskow* (formerly *Zubatka*) and *Nizhni-Novgorod* (formerly *Okun*). The former was launched in June 1988, the latter in July 1992. The Sierra II (Type 9456A Kondor class) boats have a diving depth of 750m (2460ft). One notable feature of the Sierras is the large space between the two hulls, which has obvious advantages for radiated noise reduction and damage resistance.

SPECIFICATIONS

COUNTRY: Russia
LAUNCH DATE: July 1986 (Tula, Sierra I class)
CREW: 61
DISPLACEMENT: surfaced 7112 tonnes (7000 tons); submerged 8230 tonnes (8100 tons)
DIMENSIONS: 107m x 12.5m x 8.8m (351ft x 41ft x 28ft 11in)
ARMAMENT: four 650mm (25.6in) and four 533mm (21in) torpedo tubes; SS-N-15 Starfish and SS-N-21 Samson SSMs
POWERPLANT: single shaft, one nuclear PWR, one turbine
RANGE: unlimited
PERFORMANCE: surfaced 10 knots; submerged 32 knots

Siroco

The Spanish Navy ordered its first two Agosta-class boats (*Galerna* and *Siroco*) in May 1975, and a second pair (*Mistral* and *Tramontana*) in June 1977. Designed by the French Directorate of Naval Construction as very quiet but high-performance ocean-going diesel-electric boats (SSKs), the Agosta-class boats are each armed with four bow torpedo tubes which are equipped with a rapid-reload pneumatic ramming system that can launch weapons with a minimum of noise signature. The tubes were of a completely new design when the Agostas were authorized in the mid-1970s, allowing a submarine to fire its weapons at all speeds and at any depth down to its maximum operational limit, which in the case of the Agostas is 350m (1148ft). The Spanish Agostas were built with some French assistance, and upgraded in the mid-1990s.

SPECIFICATIONS

COUNTRY: Spain
LAUNCH DATE: 13 November 1982
CREW: 54
DISPLACEMENT: surfaced 1514 tonnes ((1490 tons); submerged 1768 tonnes (1740 tons)
DIMENSIONS: 67.6m x 6.8m x 5.4m (221ft 9in x 22ft 4 in x 17ft 9in)
ARMAMENT: four 550mm (21.7in) torpedo tubes; 40 mines
POWERPLANT: two diesels, one electric motor
RANGE: not known
PERFORMANCE: surfaced 12.5 knots; submerged 17.5 knots

Sjöormen

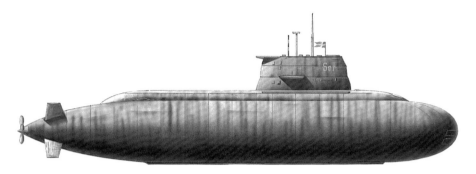

The six boats of the Sjoormen class were the first modern-type submarines to enter service with the Royal Swedish Navy. They were designed in the early 1960s and construction was equally divided between Kockums of Malmø (the designer) and Karlskrona Varvet. With an Albacore-type hull for speed and a twin-deck arrangement, the class was extensively used in the relatively shallow Baltic, where its excellent manoeuvrability and silent-running capabilities greatly enhanced the Swedish Navy's ASW operations. All six boats were upgraded in 1984–85 with new Ericsson IBS-A17 combat data/fire control systems. In the 1990s they were progressively replaced by the new A19 class, which incorporate a fully integrated combat system, more extensive sensors and even quieter machinery to allow their use on offensive (hunter-killer) ASW patrols.

SPECIFICATIONS

COUNTRY: Sweden
LAUNCH DATE: 25 January 1967
CREW: 18
DISPLACEMENT: surfaced 1143 tonnes (1125 tons); submerged 1422 tonnes (1400 tons)
DIMENSIONS: 51m x 6.1m x 5.8m (167ft 3in x 20ft x 19ft)
ARMAMENT: four 533mm (21in) and two 400mm (15.75in) torpedo tubes
POWERPLANT: single shaft, four diesels, one electric motor
RANGE: not known
PERFORMANCE: surfaced 15 knots; submerged 20 knots

Skate

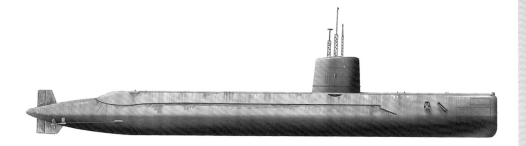

Laid down in July 1955, the USS *Skate* was the world's first production-model nuclear submarine, followed by three more boats of her class, *Swordfish*, *Sargo* and *Seadragon*. *Skate* made the first completely submerged Atlantic crossing. In 1958 she established a (then) record of 31 days submerged with a sealed atmosphere; on 11 August 1958 she passed under the North Pole during an Arctic cruise; and on 17 March 1959 she became the first submarine to surface at the North Pole. Other boats of the class also achieved notable 'firsts'; in August 1960, *Seadragon* made a transit from the Atlantic to the Pacific via the Northwest Passage (Lancaster Sound, Barrow and McClure Straits). In August 1962 *Skate*, operating from New London, Connecticut, and *Seadragon*, based at Pearl Harbor, made rendezvous under the North Pole.

SPECIFICATIONS

COUNTRY: United States
LAUNCH DATE: 16 May 1967
CREW: 95
DISPLACEMENT: surfaced 2611 tonnes (2570 tons); submerged 2907 tonnes (2861 tons)
DIMENSIONS: 81.5m x 7.6m x 6.4m (267 ft 8in x 24ft 11in x 21ft)
ARMAMENT: six 533mm (21in) torpedo tubes
POWERPLANT: two shafts, one nuclear PWR, turbines
RANGE: unlimited
PERFORMANCE: surfaced 20 knots; submerged 25 knots

Skipjack

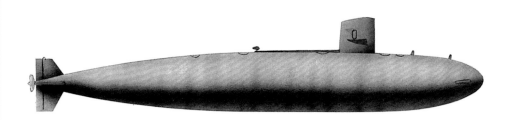

The USS *Skipjack* (SSN 585) was class leader of a group of six nuclear attack submarines built in the late 1950s. The other members of the class were *Scamp* (SSN 588), *Scorpion* (SSN 589), *Sculpin* (SSN 590), *Shark* (SSN 591) and *Snook* (SSN 592). In May 1968, *Scorpion* was lost with all 99 crew members on board some 740km (400nm) southwest of the Azores while en route from the Mediterranean to her base at Norfolk, Virginia. The original *Scorpion* was renumbered SSBN 598 and built as the nuclear ballistic-missile submarine *George Washington*. Until the advent of the Los Angeles class, the Skipjacks were the fastest submarines available to the US Navy, and had a crucial role to play in the detection, pursuit and destruction of missile submarines from an opposing fleet.

SPECIFICATIONS

COUNTRY: United States
LAUNCH DATE: 26 May 1958
CREW: 106–114
DISPLACEMENT: surfaced 3124 tonnes (3075 tons); submerged 3556 tonnes (3500 tons)
DIMENSIONS: 76.7m x 9.6m x 8.5m (251ft 9in x 31ft 6in x 27ft 10in)
ARMAMENT: six 533mm (21in) torpedo tubes
POWERPLANT: single shaft, one nuclear PWR, two steam turbines
RANGE: unlimited
PERFORMANCE: surfaced 18 knots; submerged 30 knots

Soryu class

The Soryu class are the largest boats built by Japan since World War II. They are diesel-electric attack subs powered by an air-independent propulsion system developed in Sweden and license-built in Japan. The extra space required for this system is one reason for the increased size over the previous Oyashio class boats. The hull is coated in anechoic tiles, with internal components mounted on vibration-damping mountings to reduce acoustic signature. The boats are capable of launching torpedoes and harpoon missiles through their tubes, and feature an X-shaped rudder, which improves manoeuvrability as well as allowing the boat to operate extremely close to the seabed. The Japanese Maritime Self-Defence Force intends to maintain a fleet of around 20 submarines, and will probably build 5–6 vessels of the Soryu class.

SPECIFICATIONS

COUNTRY: Japan
LAUNCH DATE: 5 December 2007
CREW: 65
DISPLACEMENT: surfaced 2900 tonnes (2854 tons); submerged 4200 tonnes (4134 tons)
DIMENSIONS: 84m x 9.1m x 8.5m (275ft 7in x 29ft 10in x 27ft 10in)
ARMAMENT: six 533mm (21in) tubes capable of launching type 89 torpedoes, sub-harpoon missiles, and mines
POWERPLANT: two Kawasaki 12V diesels; Kawasaki 4V-275R AIP engine
RANGE: 12,038km (6500nm) at 6.4 knots using AIP propulsion
PERFORMANCE: surfaced 13 knots; submerged 20 knots

Spearfish torpedo

Designed to meet Naval Staff requirement 7525, the Marconi Spearfish is an advanced-capabilities wire-guided dual-role heavyweight torpedo. It was a product of the Cold War, intended to engage the new generation of high-speed deep-diving Russian submarines with the help of its HAP-Otto fuel-powered Sundstrand 21TP01 gas turbine engine with a pump-jet outlet that can drive it to speeds in excess of 60 knots. The warhead is of the directed-energy shaped-charge type, designed to penetrate Russian double-hulled submarines such as the *Oscar* SSGN and *Typhoon* SSBN. A computer enables the torpedo to make its own tactical decisions during an engagement. Work on the development prototypes began in 1982, the first in-water trials taking place the following year, and the weapon became operational in 1988.

SPECIFICATIONS

COUNTRY: United Kingdom
LAUNCH DATE: n/a
CREW: n/a
DISPLACEMENT: n/a
DIMENSIONS: 533mm x 8.5m (21in x 27ft 11in)
ARMAMENT: n/a
POWERPLANT: n/a
RANGE: 36.5km (19.7nm)
PERFORMANCE: 65 knots

SS-N-18

The SS-N-18 (NATO designation Stingray) is a fifth-generation, two-stage, liquid-fuel SLBM; it was the first Russian SLBM to have multiple warheads and was deployed in three versions, two with MIRVs and one with a single warhead. The SS-N-18 Mod 1 version was the first Soviet SLBM to feature MIRV capability. The missile was deployed on 14 Delta III class SSBNs and first became operational in 1977–78. The Mod 2 missiles carry a large single warhead with a yield of 4.5mT. The missile has a stellar inertial guidance system with the capacity for multiple star sightings; CEP is 900m (3000ft). Each Delta III SSBN carries 16 missiles. As each of these craft was commissioned and deployed from 1976 to 1978, the Russians progressively withdrew their Yankee SSBNs from service. Russian designation of the SS-N-18 is RSM-50.

SPECIFICATIONS

COUNTRY: Russia
LAUNCH DATE: n/a
CREW: n/a
DISPLACEMENT: n/a
DIMENSIONS: 1.8m x 14m (5ft 11in x 46ft)
ARMAMENT: n/a
POWERPLANT: n/a
RANGE: 8000km (4312nm)
PERFORMANCE: not known

SS-N-20

The SS-N-20, allocated the NATO code-name Sturgeon, was the Soviet Union's first solid-fuel SLBM to be armed with MIRVs. A three-stage missile, it was deployed on the Soviet Navy's five operational Typhoon-class submarines and a single Golf V test submarine. Each missile was counted as carrying ten 100/200kT independently-targeted re-entry vehicles under agreed US and Soviet counting rules for the Strategic Arms Limitation Treaty (START) negotiations. The SS-N-20 is inertially guided and has an accuracy (circular error of probability/CEP) of about 600m (1800ft). Its range of 8300km (5160 miles) allows the submarine to fire the weapon from within the Arctic circle and still hit a target within continental US. Four test flights in 1980 were failures, followed by two sucessful tests in 1981. The SS-N-20 system became operational in 1983.

SPECIFICATIONS

COUNTRY: Russia
LAUNCH DATE: n/a
CREW: n/a
DISPLACEMENT: n/a
DIMENSIONS: 2.2m x15m (7ft 2in x 49ft)
ARMAMENT: n/a
POWERPLANT: n/a
RANGE: 8300km (4473nm)
PERFORMANCE: not known

SS-N-6

During 1961–62, fresh impetus was given to the Soviet sea-based strategic missile programme, partly in response to the rapid deployment of the US Polaris submarine force. The Yankee class SSBNs, probably originally intended as the platform for the SS-NX-13 anti-carrier ballistic missile (tested from 1970 to 1973, but never deployed) was redirected to carry 16 SS-N-6 missiles, a design derived from the SS-11 ICBM. The SS-N-6, codenamed Sawfly by NATO, was a vast improvement over the SSN-5; it had almost twice the range, 50 per cent greater accuracy, and improved reliability. Nevertheless, its range was still limited, making it necessary for the Yankee boats (deployed from 1974) to be stationed well forward in their Atlantic and Pacific patrol areas. The deployments ceased in 1987.

SPECIFICATIONS

COUNTRY: Russia
LAUNCH DATE: n/a
CREW: n/a
DISPLACEMENT: n/a
DIMENSIONS: 1.6m x 9.65m (5ft 3in x 31ft 7in)
ARMAMENT: n/a
POWERPLANT: n/a
RANGE: 3000km (1617nm)
PERFORMANCE: not known

Sting Ray torpedo

Designed to supplement the American Mk 46 Mod 2 and to replace the Mk 44 torpedoes in British service, the Sting Ray lightweight torpedo was the sequel to the abortive MoD in-house Mk 30 and 31 programmes, cancelled in 1970. Sting Ray is the first British torpedo to be developed entirely by private industry and incorporates a number of technical innovations. The weapon is capable of being launched from helicopters, aircraft and surface ships over a wide range of speeds and sea states and, as a result of its unique guidance system, can be used satisfactorily in both shallow and deep waters with a high single-shot kill probability. The former was demonstrated when a Sting Ray dropped by a Nimrod aircraft of No 42 (TB) squadron sank the decommissioned submarine *Porpoise*, moored at periscope depth.

SPECIFICATIONS

COUNTRY: United Kingdom
LAUNCH DATE: n/a
CREW: n/a
DISPLACEMENT: n/a
DIMENSIONS: 324mm x 2.6m (12.75in x 8ft 6in)
ARMAMENT: n/a
POWERPLANT: n/a
RANGE: 11.1km (6 nm)
PERFORMANCE: 45 knots

Storm

Storm was in the second group of S class boats, laid down in 1942–43. Of the 50 boats in this group, nine were lost in World War II. *Sahib* was sunk by the Italian corvette *Gabbiano* on 24 April 1943; *Saracen* was sunk by the Italian corvette *Minerva* off Bastia on 18 August 1943; P222 (unnamed) was sunk by the Italian torpedo boat *Fortunale* off Naples on 12 December 1942; *Sickle* was mined in the eastern Mediterranean on or about 18 June 1944; *Simoom* was probably sunk by *U565* in the Dodecanese on 15 November 1943; *Splendid* was sunk by the German destroyer *Hermes* off Corsica on 21 April 1943; *Stonehenge* disappeared off the Nicobar Islands on 22 March 1944; *Stratagem* was sunk by a Japanese patrol off Malacca on 22 November 1944; and *Syrtis* was mined off Bodó, Norway, on 28 March 1944. *Storm* was scrapped in 1949.

SPECIFICATIONS

COUNTRY: United Kingdom
LAUNCH DATE: 18 May 1943
CREW: 44
DISPLACEMENT: surfaced 726 tonnes (715 tons); submerged 1006 tonnes (990 tons)
DIMENSIONS: 61.8m x 7.25m x 3.2m (202ft 6in x 23ft 9in x 10ft 6in)
ARMAMENT: six 533mm (21in) torpedo tubes; one 76mm (3in) gun
POWERPLANT: twin screws, diesel/electric motors
RANGE: 15,750km (8500nm) at 10 knots
PERFORMANCE: surfaced 14.75 knots; submerged 9 knots

Sturgeon

An enlarged and improved Thresher/
Permit design with additional
quieting features and electronic systems,
the Sturgeon-class SSNs built between
1965 and 1974 were the largest class
of nuclear-powered warships until the
advent of the Los Angeles class. The
Sturgeons have been frequently used in
the intelligence-gathering role, carrying
special equipment and National Security
Agency personnel. All 37 Stugeon-class
boats were still in service in the 1990s.
In 1982, *Cavalla* was converted at Pearl
Harbor to have a secondary amphibious
assault role by carrying a swimmer delivery
vehicle (SDV); *Archerfish*, *Silversides*,
Tunny and *L. Mendel Rivers* are similarly
equipped. *William H. Bates*, *Hawkbill*,
Pintado, *Richard B. Russell* and others
have been modified to carry and support
the Navy's Deep Submergence and Rescue
vehicles.

SPECIFICATIONS

COUNTRY: United States
LAUNCH DATE: 26 February 1966
CREW: 121–141
DISPLACEMENT: surfaced 4335 tonnes (4266 tons);
submerged 4854 tonnes (4777 tons)
DIMENSIONS: 89m x 9.65m x 8.9m (292ft 3in x 31ft
8in x 29ft 3in)
ARMAMENT: four 533mm (21in) torpedo tubes;
Tomahawk & sub harpoon SSMs
POWERPLANT: single shaft, one nuclear PWR,
turbines
RANGE: unlimited
PERFORMANCE: surfaced 18 knots; submerged
26 knots

Sub-Martel

Sub-Martel, properly designated Under-Sea Guided Weapon CL137, was a unilateral attempt by the UK to develop an effective submarine-launched SSM to counter the Russian N-7 system. It was to have been a collaborative effort between HSD and the French firm Matra – designers of the air-launched version – but this scheme was abandoned when the French turned their attention to development of the SM38 Exocet. The USGW was based heavily on Martel, but Matra took no part in the project. The intention was to extend the length of the Martel body and add folding flip-out wings and a booster motor. The homing head was to be developed by Marconi Space and Defence Systems. In the event, development was cancelled in 1975, after some £16 million had been spent, and orders were placed for the American Harpoon SSM instead.

SPECIFICATIONS

COUNTRY: United Kingdom
LAUNCH DATE: n/a
CREW: n/a
DISPLACEMENT: n/a
DIMENSIONS: 400mm x 3.87m (15.75in x 152.4in)
ARMAMENT: n/a
POWERPLANT: n/a
RANGE: 30km (16nm)
PERFORMANCE: not known

Swiftsure

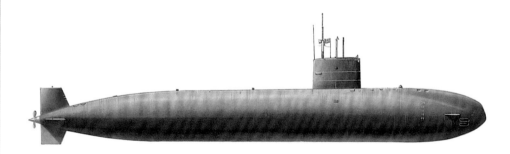

There were six boats in this SSN class, which were completed between July 1974 and March 1981; *Swiftsure*, *Sovereign*, *Superb*, *Sceptre*, *Spartan* and *Splendid*. All underwent major refits in the late 1970s or early 1990s, with a full tactical weapons system upgrade. Each was fitted with a PWR 1 Core Z, providing a 12-year life cycle, although refits remain on an eight-year schedule. As a result of budget cuts, *Swiftsure* was paid off in 1992, but the others were still operational in 1999. Two of the class are usually in refit or maintenance. *Splendid* was the first British submarine to carry a warload of Tomahawk cruise missiles, and used them in the 1999 NATO strikes on Serbia. The sonar fit is the Type 2074 (active/passive search and attack), Type 2007 (passive), Type 2046 (towed array), 2019 (intercept and ranging) and Type 2077 (short range classification).

SPECIFICATIONS

COUNTRY: United Kingdom
LAUNCH DATE: 07 September 1971
CREW: 116
DISPLACEMENT: surfaced 4471 tonnes (4400 tons); submerged 4979 tonnes (4900 tons)
DIMENSIONS: 82.9m x 9.8m x 8.5m (272ft x 32ft 4in x 28ft)
ARMAMENT: five 533mm (21in) torpedo tubes; Tomahawk and sub harpoon SSMs
POWERPLANT: single shaft, nuclear PWR, turbines
RANGE: unlimited
PERFORMANCE: surfaced 20 knots; submerged 30 plus knots

Tang

The US Navy's Tang class of diesel-electric attack submarines – the equivalents of Russia's Whiskey class – embodied many lessons gleaned from the German Type XXI U-boats. The first four were engined with a new type of radial diesel which caused a lot of problems in service, so they were later re-engined with more conventional motors. The class was conceived virtually on an experimental basis, the US Navy being anxious to discover what improvements could be embodied into a new class of boat in the light of wartime experience and technical advances, but in the event it formed the basis of further postwar development. The six boats in the class were *Trigger* (sold to Italy as the *Livio Piomarto* in 1974), *Wahoo*, *Trout*, *Gudgeon* and *Harder* (sold to Italy as the *Romeo Romei* in 1973). *Tang* was sold to Turkey as the *Piri Reis* in 1980.

SPECIFICATIONS

COUNTRY: United States
LAUNCH DATE: 19 June 1951
CREW: 83
DISPLACEMENT: surfaced 1585 tonnes (1560 tons); submerged 2296 tonnes (2260 tons)
DIMENSIONS: 82m x 8.3m x 5.2m (269ft 2in x 27ft 2in x 17ft 1in)
ARMAMENT: eight 533mm (21in) torpedo tubes
POWERPLANT: twin shafts, diesel/electric motors
RANGE: 18,530km (10,000nm) at 10 knots
PERFORMANCE: surfaced 15.5 knots; submerged 18.3 knots

Tango

The Tango class of 18 diesel-electric attack submarines was built as an interim measure, filling the gap between the Foxtrot class DE boats and the Victor nuclear-powered SSNs. The first unit was completed at Gorky in 1972 and, over the next ten years, 17 more units were built in two slightly different versions. The later type were several metres longer than the first in order to accommodate the fire-control systems associated with the tube-launched SS-N-15 anti-submarine missile, the equivalent of the US Navy's SUBROC. The bow sonar installations were the same as those fitted to later Soviet SSNs, while the powerplant was identical to that installed in the later units of the Foxtrot class. Production of the Tango class ceased after the 18th unit was built; six were still in service early in 1999, the rest having been paid off.

SPECIFICATIONS

COUNTRY: Russia
LAUNCH DATE: 1971
CREW: 60
DISPLACEMENT: surfaced 3251 tonnes (3200 tons); submerged 3962 tonnes (3900 tons)
DIMENSIONS: 92m x 9m x 7m (301ft 10in x 29ft 6in x 23ft)
ARMAMENT: six 533mm (21in) torpedo tubes
POWERPLANT: not known
RANGE: twin screws, diesel/electric motors
PERFORMANCE: surfaced 20 knots; submerged 16 knots

Thomson-Sintra sea mine

Thomson-Sintra produces two types of operational sea mine. The TSM5310 is an offensive ground mine fitted with a multi-sensor fusing system based on two or all of the magnetic, acoustic and pressure actuating influences, and is shaped for launching from the torpedo tube of a submarine. The sensitivity of the fusing can be adjusted before laying to suit the depth of water and the type of target likely to be encountered. The mine is armed by withdrawing two pins before it is loaded into the tube and is activated by a pre-set timing delay to allow the submarine to clear the area. The other mine – the TSM3530 – is a defensive mine deployed from surface vessels fitted with mine rails. Both mines are in service with the French Navy and have been widely exported, especially to those countries that have purchased Daphne-class submarines.

SPECIFICATIONS
COUNTRY: France
LAUNCH DATE: n/a
CREW: n/a
DISPLACEMENT: n/a
DIMENSIONS: 0.53m (1ft 10in)
ARMAMENT: n/a
POWERPLANT: n/a
RANGE: not known
PERFORMANCE: not known

Thresher/Permit class

The first of the SSNs in the US Navy with a deep-diving capability, advanced sonars mounted in the optimum bow position, amidships angled torpedo tubes with the SUBROC ASW missile, and a high degree of machinery-quieting, the Thresher class formed an important part of the US subsurface attack capability for 20 years. The lead boat, USS *Thresher*, was lost with all 129 crew on board, off New England on 10 April 1963, midway through the building period of 1960–66. The class was then renamed after *Permit*, the second ship. As a result of the enquiry following the loss of *Thresher*, the last three of the class were modified during construction with SUBSAFE features. The names of the class were *Permit*, *Plunger*, *Barb*, *Pollack*, *Haddo*, *Guardfish*, *Flasher* and *Haddock* (Pacific Fleet); and *Jack*, *Tinosa*, *Dace*, *Greenling* and *Gato* (Atlantic Fleet).

SPECIFICATIONS

COUNTRY: United States
LAUNCH DATE: 9 July 1960 (Thresher)
CREW: 134–141
DISPLACEMENT: surfaced 3810 tonnes (3750 tons); submerged 4380 tonnes (4311 tons)
DIMENSIONS: 84.9m x 9.6m x 8.8m (278ft 6in x 31ft 8in x 28ft 10in)
ARMAMENT: four 533mm (21in) torpedo tubes
POWERPLANT: single shaft, one nuclear PWR, steam turbines
RANGE: unlimited
PERFORMANCE: surfaced 18 knots; submerged 27 knots

Tigerfish torpedo

T he origins of the Mk 24 Tigerfish heavyweight torpedo can be found as far back as 1959 in a British torpedo project codenamed 'Ongar'. By 1970, it was realized that the technology involved could not be handled solely by an in-house service approach, so the (then) Marconi company was given the job of developing the weapon from 1972 onwards. This was five years after the originally envisaged in-service date. As a result of development and engineering problems the first version of the Tigerfish, the Mk 24 Mod 0, entered fleet service in 1974 with less than adequate operational capability. It was only granted its full Fleet Weapon Acceptance certificate in 1979, after protracted evaluation. To rectify the problems Marconi initiated development of the Mk 24 Mod 1, but they were not entirely solved until the emergence of Mk 24 Mod 2 in 1986.

SPECIFICATIONS

COUNTRY: United Kingdom
LAUNCH DATE: n/a
CREW: n/a
DISPLACEMENT: n/a
DIMENSIONS: 533m x 6.4m (21in x 21ft 2in)
ARMAMENT: n/a
POWERPLANT: n/a
RANGE: 29km (15.6nm)
PERFORMANCE: 35 knots

Torbay

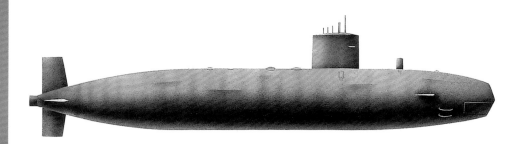

HMS *Torbay* is the fourth boat of the Trafalgar-class SSNs, the lead ship of which was ordered on 7 April 1977 and launched on 1 July 1981. The other vessels in the class are *Turbulent* (launched 1 December 1982), *Tireless* (17 March 1984), *Trenchant* (3 November 1986), *Talent* (15 April 1988) and *Triumph* (16 February 1991). HMS *Trafalgar* was a trials submarine for the Spearfish torpedo, which went into full production in 1992 and was first deployed in Trenchant early in 1994. The submarines' pressure hulls and outer surfaces are covered with conformal anechoic coatings to reduce noise, and as a further noise reduction measure the main propulsion and auxiliary machinery are suspended from transverse bulkheads. All the vessels are in service with the 2nd Submarine Squadron at Devonport, and two are usually in refit at any time.

SPECIFICATIONS

COUNTRY: United Kingdom
LAUNCH DATE: 8 March 1985
CREW: 130
DISPLACEMENT: surfaced 4877 tonnes (4800 tons); submerged 5384 tonnes (5300 tons)
DIMENSIONS: 85.4m x 10m x 8.2m (280ft 2in x 33ft 2in x 27ft)
ARMAMENT: five 533mm (21in) torpedo tubes; Tomahawk and sub harpoon SSMs
POWERPLANT: pump jet, one PWR, turbines
RANGE: unlimited
PERFORMANCE: surfaced 20 knots; submerged 32 knots

Trafalgar

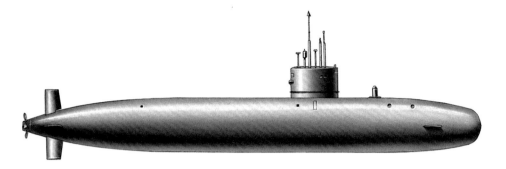

Essentially an improved Swiftsure, HMS *Trafalgar* and her sister ships consitute the third generation of British SSNs to be built by Vickers Shipbuilding and Engineering Ltd (VSEL) at Barrow-in-Furness. Improvements included a new reactor system and a pump-jet propulsion system in place of a conventional propeller. *Trafalgar* was the first boat to be fitted with the Type 2020 sonar, and was used as development test platform. The deployment of the Trafalgar class brought the Royal Navy's SSN fleet to 12 boats by the mid-1990s, a lean but highly effective force. The end of the Cold War and increasing global instability has led to the widespread dispersal of the RN's SSNs; for example, in 1995, HMS *Trenchant*'s operational programme took her to Guam, Singapore, Hong Kong, Diego Garcia and South Korea.

SPECIFICATIONS

COUNTRY: United Kingdom
LAUNCH DATE: 1 July 1981
CREW: 130
DISPLACEMENT: surfaced 4877 tonnes (4800 tons); submerged 5384 tonnes (5300 tons)
DIMENSIONS: 85.4m x 10m x 8.2m (280ft 2in x 33ft 2in x 27ft)
ARMAMENT: five 533mm (21in) torpedo tubes; Tomahawk and sub harpoon SSMs
POWERPLANT: pump jet, one PWR, turbines
RANGE: unlimited
PERFORMANCE: surfaced 20 knots; submerged 32 knots

Triton

USS *Triton* was designed and built for use as a radar picket submarine to operate in conjunction with surface carrier task forces, submerging only when in danger of enemy attack. For this purpose, she was fitted with an elaborate combat information centre and a large radar antenna that retracted into her sail. At that time, she was the longest submarine ever built, and was exceeded in displacement only by the later Polaris SSBNs. In 1960, *Triton* circumnavigated the globe entirely underwater, except for one instance when her sail structure broke surface to allow a sick submariner to be taken off near the Falkland Islands. The 66,749km (36,022nm) cruise took 83 days and was made at an average speed of 18 knots. On 1 March 1961, *Triton* was reclassified as an attack submarine. She was decommissioned on 3 May 1969.

SPECIFICATIONS

COUNTRY: United States
LAUNCH DATE: 19 August 1958
CREW: 172
DISPLACEMENT: surfaced 6035 tonnes (5940 tons); submerged 7905 tonnes (7780 tons)
DIMENSIONS: 136.3m x 11.3m x 7.3m (447ft 6in x 37ft 1in x 24ft)
ARMAMENT: six 533mm (21in) torpedo tubes
POWERPLANT: two shafts, one nuclear PWR, turbines
RANGE: unlimited
PERFORMANCE: surfaced 27 knots; submerged 20 knots

Type 039 Song Class

The Type 039, China's first indigenous submarine class, replaced the Ming class, itself an improved version of the Russian Romeo class. It uses an upgraded version of the command and control system installed in the Ming class. The Song Class is a diesel-electric boat intended for anti-ship and anti-submarine work, but capable of other duties, such as mine-laying. For this mission, the boats carry 24–36 mines in place of their torpedoes and emplace them using the torpedo tubes. The Type 039 was the first boat to use a teardrop-shaped hull, but development was problematic. Between launch and commissioning in 1999, the lead boat was redesigned to eliminate problems with performance and acoustic signature. This version is designated Type 039G, with the Type 039G1 version incorporating further improvements. The hull is coated in anechoic tiles, which reduce detection range.

SPECIFICATIONS

COUNTRY: China
LAUNCH DATE: 1998
CREW: 60
DISPLACEMENT: surfaced 1700 tonnes (1673 tons); submerged 2250 tonnes (2214 tons)
DIMENSIONS: 75m x 8.4m x 5.3m (246ft x 27.5ft x 17.4ft)
ARMAMENT: six 533mm torpedo tubes capable of launching Yu-3 anti-submarine torpedoes, Yu-4 anti-ship torpedoes and YJ-8 anti-ship missiles
POWERPLANT: three MTU 16V396SE84 diesels
RANGE: not known
PERFORMANCE: surfaced 15 knots; submerged 22 knots

Type 093

The Type 093 class was developed to replace the preceding Type 091 class of nuclear attack submarines, but was plagued with design problems. Rumours that Russian assistance helped overcome difficulties with the powerplant and other systems have never been confirmed. The whole project was subject to tight security, especially during sea trials that lasted from 2002 to 2006. As a result of the secrecy surrounding the project, little is known about the Type 093. The boat's characteristics allow an estimate, which is thought to be equivalent to early versions of the Los Angeles class. It has six torpedo tubes capable of launching anti-ship and anti-submarine torpedoes, or missiles for a standoff anti-ship attack. There are also unconfirmed reports that land-attack cruise missiles can be launched. Although inferior to first-line Western submarines, the Type 093 represents a major increase in Chinese naval capabilities.

SPECIFICATIONS

COUNTRY: China
LAUNCH DATE: December 2002
CREW: not known, probably 100–120
DISPLACEMENT: estimated at 6000–7000 tonnes (5905–6889 tons) submerged
DIMENSIONS: 110m x 11m x 10m (361ft x 36ft x 32.8ft)
ARMAMENT: six 533mm torpedo tubes; mix of anti-ship and anti-submarine torpedoes plus anti-ship missiles
POWERPLANT: high-temperature gas-cooled reactor
RANGE: effectively unlimited
PERFORMANCE: surfaced not known; submerged estimated 35 knots

Type 214 (Papanikolis U214)

The Type 214 class is a development of the successful Type 212 class. Type 214 boats have been purchased by Turkey, Pakistan and South Korea, in addition to a variant named the Papanikolis class built for the Greek navy. The Type 214 class uses AIP (air-independent propulsion), which allows it to spend long periods submerged. This gives many advantages of nuclear propulsion without the associated technical and political issues. The first Greek Type 214 was built in Germany, with follow-on vessels constructed in Greek yards. However, the lead boat ran into difficulties at the acceptance stage, requiring further sea trials and delaying its commissioning into the Greek navy. The Type 214 is armed with eight torpedo tubes, of which four can launch Harpoon missiles. All tubes can launch Black Shark dual-purpose wire-guided torpedoes, which can be used to attack surface or submarine targets.

SPECIFICATIONS

COUNTRY: Greece
LAUNCH DATE: April 2004
CREW: 27
DISPLACEMENT: surfaced 1690 tonnes (1663 tons); submerged 1860 tonnes (1831 tons)
DIMENSIONS: 64m x 6.3m x 6m (210ft x 20.7ft x 19.7ft)
ARMAMENT: four 533mm (21in) torpedo tubes; 24 torpedoes carried. Four tubes are capable of launching Harpoon missiles
POWERPLANT: one MTU 16V-396 diesel engine (3.12MW); Siemens AIP (Air-Independent Propulsion) (300kW)
RANGE: 12,000nm
PERFORMANCE: surfaced 12 knots; submerged 6 knots cruising; 20 knots sprint

Type 640

The Type 640 is one of many variants of the well-proven German Type 205/206 SSK design. Built for the Israeli Navy (Hel Yam) by Vickers Ltd at Barrow-in-Furness in the UK in the mid-1970s, following a contract signed in April 1972, this particular sub-class is designed specifically for coastal operations. Three boats were involved in the deal; the first, *Gal*, was laid down in 1973 and commissioned in December 1976. The other two boats, *Tanin* and *Rahav*, were commissioned in June and December 1977 respectively. The boats were re-designated Type 540 in Israeli service. The boats are built of high-tensile nonmagnetic steel. They are intended purely for export, and each country can choose its own equipment fit depending on the funding available. This class of boat is ideal for operation in the fairly shallow waters of the Levant.

SPECIFICATIONS

COUNTRY: Israel
LAUNCH DATE: 2 December 1975 (class leader)
CREW: 22
DISPLACEMENT: surfaced 427 tonnes (420 tons); submerged 610 tonnes (600 tons)
DIMENSIONS: 45m x 4.7m x 3.7m (147ft 8in x 15ft 5in x 12ft 2in)
ARMAMENT: eight 533mm (21in) torpedo tubes
POWERPLANT: single shaft, two diesels, one electric motor
RANGE: 7038km (3800nm) at 10 knots
PERFORMANCE: surfaced 11 knots; submerged 17 knots

Typhoon

Capable of hitting strategic targets anywhere in the world with its Makayev SSN-20 Sturgeon three-stage solid fuel missiles, each of which has 10,200kT nuclear warheads and a range of 8300km (4500nm), Typhoon is the largest class of submarine ever built. The launch tubes are positioned forward in the bow section, leaving space abaft the fin for two nuclear reactors. The fin can break through ice up to 3m (9ft 10in) thick, and diving depth is in the order of 300m (1000ft). Six Typhoons were commissioned between 1980 and 1989; their designations, in order, are TK208, TK202, TK12, TK13, TK17 and TK20. Two were laid up in reserve in 1999; two more were awaiting refit and unlikely to go to sea again. TK17 was damaged by fire in a missile loading accident in 1992 but was subsequently repaired. The Typhoons are based in the Northern Fleet at Litsauba.

SPECIFICATIONS

COUNTRY: Russia
LAUNCH DATE: 23 September 1980
CREW: 175
DISPLACEMENT: surfaced 18,797 tonnes (18,500 tons); submerged 26,925 tonnes (26,500 tons)
DIMENSIONS: 171.5m x 24.6m x 13m (562ft 7in x 80ft 7in x 42ft 6in)
ARMAMENT: 20 SLBMs; four 630mm (25in) and two 533mm (21in) torpedo tubes
POWERPLANT: two shafts, two nuclear PWR, turbines
RANGE: unlimited
PERFORMANCE: surfaced 12 knots; submerged 25 knots

U12

U12 was the last of the German Federal Republic's Type 205 coastal submarines, the fourth such class to become operational since the FDR rearmed as part of NATO in the 1950s. The first was the Hai (Shark) class, comprising that boat and the *Hecht* (Pike), both of which were reconstructed World War II Type XXIII U-boats. These were followed by the Types 201 and 202. With the exception of two boats, all were to have been of the Type 201 model, but there were severe hull corrosion problems, the non-magnetic material used proving quite unsatisfactory. As an interim measure, the hulls of *U4* to *U8* were covered in tin – suffering severe operational limitations as a consequence – and construction of *U9* to *U12* was suspended until a special non-magnetic steel could be developed.

SPECIFICATIONS

COUNTRY: Germany
LAUNCH DATE: 10 September 1968
CREW: 21
DISPLACEMENT: surfaced 425 tonnes (419 tons); submerged 457 tonnes (450 tons)
DIMENSIONS: 43.9m x 4.6m x 4.3m (144ft x 15ft 1in x 14ft 1in)
ARMAMENT: eight 533mm (21in) torpedo tubes
POWERPLANT: single screw, diesel/electric motors
RANGE: 7041km (3800nm) at 10 knots
PERFORMANCE: surfaced 10 knots; submerged 17.5 knots

U28

Studies for a replacement submarine to follow the Type 205 class were initiated in 1962. The result was the new Type 206 class which, built of high-tensile non-magnetic steel, was to be used for coastal operations and had to conform with treaty limitations on the maximum tonnage allowed to West Germany. New safety devices for the crew were fitted, and the armament fit permitted the carriage of wire-guided torpedoes. After final design approval had been given, construction planning took place in 1966–68, and the first orders (for an eventual total of 18 units) were placed in the following year. By 1975, all the vessels (*U13* to *U30*) were in service. The submarines were later fitted with two external containers for the carriage of up to 24 ground mines in addition to their torpedo armament.

SPECIFICATIONS

COUNTRY: Germany
LAUNCH DATE: 22 January 1974
CREW: 21
DISPLACEMENT: surfaced 457 tonnes (450 tons); submerged 508 tonnes (500 tons)
DIMENSIONS: 48.6m x 4.6m x 4.5m (159 ft 5in x 15ft 2in x 14ft 10in)
ARMAMENT: eight 533mm (21in) torpedo tubes
POWERPLANT: single shaft, diesel/electric motors
RANGE: 7041km (3800nm) at 10 knots
PERFORMANCE: surfaced 10 knots; submerged 17 knots

U1081

The *U1081* was leader of a planned class of ten Type XVIIG coastal U-boats powered by the revolutionary Walter geared turbine, but still fitted with diesel/electric drive to extend their radius of action. The Type XVIIG class were generally similar to the Type XVIIB, although about 1.5m (5ft) shorter. A further class of experimental boats, the Type XVIIK, was planned for the purpose of testing the closed-cycle diesel engine as an alternative to the Walter turbine, but like the XVIIG it never advanced beyond project status. Three XVIIBs were built, all being scuttled in May 1945. One of them, the *U1407*, was salved, repaired and allocated to the Royal Navy under the name Meteorite. She was used to make exhaustive tests of the Walter propulsion system and was scrapped in 1950. Had they become available, the Type XV11s would have been formidable opponents.

SPECIFICATIONS

COUNTRY: Germany
LAUNCH DATE: project cancelled (1945)
CREW: 19
DISPLACEMENT: surfaced 319 tonnes (314 tons); submerged 363 tonnes (357 tons)
DIMENSIONS: 40.5m x 3.3m x 4.3m (129ft 6in x 10ft 9in x 14ft 1in)
ARMAMENT: two 533mm (21in) torpedo tubes
POWERPLANT: single-shaft geared turbine; diesel/electric motors
RANGE: not known
PERFORMANCE: surfaced 23 knots (estimated); submerged 8.5 knots

U2326

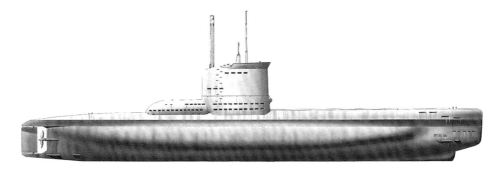

In the latter months of World War II, Germany launched a massive submarine construction programme, the aim of which was to get two types of submarine – the Type XXI and Type XXIII – into service as quickly as possible. Both were fitted with diesel/electric motors, plus electric 'creeping' motors that made them extremely hard to detect. The *U2326* was a Type XXIII U-boat, one of 57 that were either at sea, in various stages of construction or projected at the end of the war in Europe. The building programme was severely disrupted by Allied bombing, and only a few Type XXIIIs were operational in the final weeks of the war. After the surrender the *U2326* went to Britain, where she was used for experimental work as the N25. She was handed over to France in 1946, and lost in an accident off Toulon in December that year.

SPECIFICATIONS

COUNTRY: Germany
LAUNCH DATE: not known
CREW: 14
DISPLACEMENT: surfaced 236 tonnes (232 tons); submerged 260 tonnes (256 tons)
DIMENSIONS: 34m x 2.9m x 3.7m (112ft x 9ft 9in x 12ft 3in)
ARMAMENT: two 533mm (21in) torpedo tubes
POWERPLANT: single-shaft diesel/electric motors; silent creeping electric motor
RANGE: 2171km (1172nm) at 7 knots
PERFORMANCE: surfaced 9.75 knots; submerged 12.5 knots

U2501

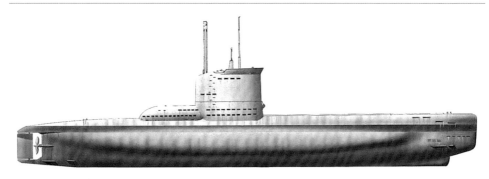

U*2501*, the first of the Type XXI ocean-going U-boats, was a milestone in the development of the submarine, a stop on the evolutionary road that led to the nuclear-powered vessels of today. She was a double-hulled vessel, with high submerged speed plus the ability to run silently at 3.5 knots on her 'creeper' electric motors. The outer hull was built of light plating to aid streamlining; the inner hull was 28–37mm (1.1–1.5in) thick carbon steel plating. She had new, super-light batteries, and could maintain a submerged speed of 16 knots for one hour; at four knots, she could remain submerged for three days on a single charge. Some 55 Type XXIs were in service when Germany surrendered in 1945, but a great many were destroyed by bombing during construction; this was fortunate for the Allies, for they were very dangerous war machines.

SPECIFICATIONS

COUNTRY: Germany
LAUNCH DATE: 1944
CREW: 57
DISPLACEMENT: surfaced 1647 tonnes (1621 tons); submerged 2100 tonnes (2067 tons)
DIMENSIONS: 77m x 8m x 6.2m (251ft 8in x 26ft 3in x 20ft 4in)
ARMAMENT: six 533mm (21in) torpedo tubes; four 30mm (1.2in) AA guns
POWERPLANT: twin screws, diesel/electric motors, silent creeping motors
RANGE: 17934km (9678nm) at 10 knots
PERFORMANCE: surfaced 15.5 knots; submerged 16 knots

U2511

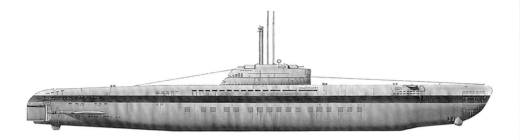

As soon as they were commissioned, the ocean-going Type XXI and the coastal Type XXIII U-boats were deployed to Norway, where it was anticipated that the German armed forces would make a last-ditch defence. The German surrender on 8 May 1945 found the Type XXI *U2511* – the first such boat to become operational in March 1945 – in the Norwegian harbour of Bergen, having just returned from a patrol in which a British cruiser was sighted on 4 May. The *U2511*'s captain – advised that the German surrender was imminent – elected to carry out only a dummy attack on the British warship, so saving its crew and probably his own. The Royal Navy knew about the Type XXIs, the deployment of which caused great concern, but they could not be brought into service fast enough before Germany's final collapse.

SPECIFICATIONS

COUNTRY: Germany
LAUNCH DATE: late 1944
CREW: 57
DISPLACEMENT: surfaced 1647 tonnes (1621 tons); submerged 2100 tonnes (2067 tons)
DIMENSIONS: 77m x 8m x 6.2m (251ft 8in x 26ft 3in x 20ft 4in)
ARMAMENT: six 533mm (21in) torpedo tubes; four 30mm (1.2in) AA guns
POWERPLANT: twin screws, diesel/electric motors, silent creeping motors
RANGE: 17,934km (9678nm) at 10 knots
PERFORMANCE: surfaced 15.5 knots; submerged 16 knots

UGM-96A Trident I C4

The purpose of the Lockheed UGM-96A Trident I C4 missile development programme was essentially to increase the range of American SLBMs to allow the use of larger and more remote patrol areas. A three-stage solid-propellant missile, Trident I was flight-tested in 1977, becoming operational two years later aboard the SSBN conversions of the Benjamin Franklin and Lafayette classes. Trident I has now been replaced by Trident II, the largest missile compatible with the launch tubes on Ohio-class SSBNs. The missile was first deployed on *Tennessee* – the ninth Ohio-class submarine – in December 1989, and a total of 312 missiles had been deployed by 1989. The missile also arms the four British Vanguard class SSBNs. In the 21st century, the American SSBN force will be a mix only of Ohio-class boats with Trident II missiles.

SPECIFICATIONS

COUNTRY: United States
LAUNCH DATE: n/a
CREW: n/a
DISPLACEMENT: n/a
DIMENSIONS: 1.89m x 10.4m (6ft 2in x 34ft 1in)
ARMAMENT: n/a
POWERPLANT: n/a
RANGE: 6808km (3669nm)
PERFORMANCE: not known

Upholder

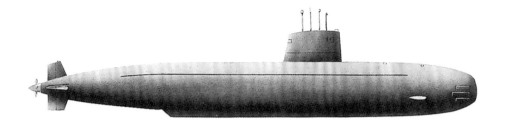

The Upholder class of four SSKs was ordered in response to an Admiralty requirement, identified in the 1970s, for a new class of diesel-electric attack submarine. The result was the Type 2400, revealed in 1979. The first boat, HMS *Upholder*, was ordered from Vickers SEL on 2 November 1983 and orders were placed for three more, named *Unseen*, *Ursula* and *Unicorn*. Plans for more of the class were dropped as part of an economic exercise. The structure comprises a single-skinned NQ1 high tensile steel hull, with a five-man lockout chamber in the fin. The boats have an endurance of 49 days, and can remain submerged for 90 hours at 3 knots. All were based at Devonport as part of the 2nd Submarine Squadron, but, by the mid-1990s, all had been placed in reserve and were awaiting disposal. There were plans in 1999 to lease or sell them to the Canadian Navy.

SPECIFICATIONS

COUNTRY: United Kingdom
LAUNCH DATE: December 1986
CREW: 47
DISPLACEMENT: surfaced 2203 tonnes (2168 tons); submerged 2494 tonnes (2455 tons)
DIMENSIONS: 70.3m x 7.6m x 5.5m (230ft 7in x 24ft 11in x 17ft 7in)
ARMAMENT: six 533mm (21in) torpedoes; sub harpoon SSMs
POWERPLANT: single shaft, diesel/electric motors
RANGE: 14,816km (8000nm) at 8 knots
PERFORMANCE: surfaced 12 knots; submerged 20 knots

V class

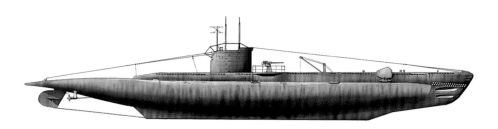

Launched in 1943–44, the Royal Navy's V-class submarines were generally similar to the U class except for their length, slightly greater because of their finer ends. In fact, the first seven boats in this category were U-class vessels, but only *Upshot* and *Urtica* were actually launched, the others being cancelled. Of the 27 boats in the class, 12 went to foreign navies before the end of the war. *Variance*, *Venturer*, *Viking* and *Votary* were allocated to the Royal Norwegian Navy as the *Utsira*, *Utstein*, *Utvaer* and *Uthaug*; *Vineyard* and *Vortex* became the French *Doris* and *Morse*; *Veldt*, *Vengeful*, *Virulent* and *Volatile* went to the Royal Hellenic Navy as the *Pipinos*, *Delfin*, *Argonaftis* and *Triaina*; while *Vulpine* was assigned to the Royal Danish Navy as the *Storen*. *Morse*, ex-*Vortex*, also went to Denmark after her French service.

SPECIFICATIONS

COUNTRY: United Kingdom
LAUNCH DATE: 19 September 1944 (HMS Vagabond)
CREW: 37
DISPLACEMENT: surfaced 554 tonnes (545 tons); submerged 752 tonnes (740 tons)
DIMENSIONS: 61m x 4.8m x 3.8m (200ft 2in x 15ft 9in x 12ft 9in)
ARMAMENT: four 533mm (21in) torpedo tubes; one 76mm (3in) gun
POWERPLANT: twin screws, diesel/electric motors
RANGE: 7041km (3800nm) at 8 knots
PERFORMANCE: surfaced 11.25 knots; submerged 9 knots

Valiant

Valiant, Britain's second nuclear submarine, was slightly larger than the first, *Dreadnought*, though of basically the same design. Like *Dreadnought*, she was built by Vickers-Armstrong. *Valiant* was originally scheduled to be completed in September 1965, but work was held up because of the priority given to the Polaris missile-armed submarines of the Resolution class, and she was not commissioned until 18 July 1966. She was followed by a sister ship, HMS *Warspite* – commissioned in April 1967 – and by three Churchill-class vessels, which were modified Valiant-class SSNs and were somewhat quieter in service, having benefited from the experience gained in operating the earlier boats. *Valiant* and *Warspite*, together with the Churchills, were paid off in the late 1980s, following the full deployment of the Trafalgar class SSNs.

SPECIFICATIONS

COUNTRY: United Kingdom
LAUNCH DATE: 3 December 1963
CREW: 116
DISPLACEMENT: surfaced 4470 tonnes (4400 tons); submerged 4979 tonnes (4900 tons)
DIMENSIONS: 86.9m x 10.1m x 8.2m (285ft 1in x 33ft 3in x 27ft)
ARMAMENT: six 533mm (21in) torpedo tubes
POWERPLANT: nuclear, one PWR
RANGE: unlimited
PERFORMANCE: surfaced 20 knots; submerged 29 knots

Vanguard

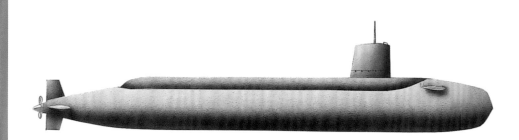

The decision to buy the US Trident I (C4) submarine-launched ballistic-missile system was announced by the UK government on 15 July 1980. A little under two years later, the government announced that it had opted for the improved Trident II system, with the more advanced D5 missile, to be deployed in four SSBNs: these would be named *Vanguard*, *Victorious*, *Vigilant* and *Vengeance*. The four British Vanguard-class Trident submarines incorporate a missile compartment based on that of the Ohio-class boats, but with 16 rather than 24 launch tubes. Trident II D5 is able to carry up to 14 warheads of 100–120kT per missile, each having sufficient accuracy to hit underground missile silos and command bunkers, but low-yield sub-strategic warheads are also carried. The Vanguards undergo a refit and refuelling every eight or nine years.

SPECIFICATIONS

COUNTRY: United Kingdom
LAUNCH DATE: 4 March 1992
CREW: 135
DISPLACEMENT: surfaced not available; submerged 16,155 tonnes (15,900 tons)
DIMENSIONS: 149.9m x 12.8m x 12m (491ft 10in x 42ft x 39ft 5in)
ARMAMENT: 16 Lockheed Trident D5 missiles; four 533mm (21in) torpedoes
POWERPLANT: one nuclear PWR; two turbines
RANGE: unlimited
PERFORMANCE: surfaced not available; submerged 25 knots

Västergötland

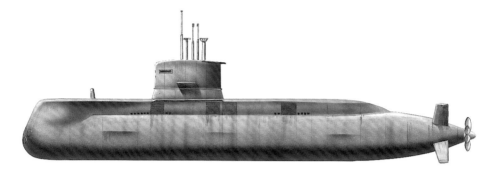

Västergötland is the lead boat of a class of four SSKs, all named after Swedish provinces. The others are *Hälsingland*, *Södermanland* and *Ostergötland*. The design contract for the class was awarded to Kockums of Malmø on 17 April 1978, and a contract for the submarines' construction followed in December 1981. The boats are optimized for operations in the Baltic, especially in shallow coastal waters. Torpedo load comprises 12 FFV Type 613 wire-guided weapons, effective to a range of 20km (10.8nm) at a speed of 45 knots, and six FFV Type 431/450, also wireguided, which are effective to a similar range. Both types of torpedo have a speed of 45 knots. It was reported that SSMs had been proposed, but that these were not considered cost-effective in the Baltic environment, where any naval engagements would be fought at fairly close range.

SPECIFICATIONS

COUNTRY: Sweden
LAUNCH DATE: 17 September 1986
CREW: 28
DISPLACEMENT: surfaced 1087 tonnes (1070 tons); submerged 1161 tonnes (1143 tons)
DIMENSIONS: 48.5m x 6.1m x 5.6m (159ft 1in x 20ft x 18ft 5in)
ARMAMENT: six 533mm (21in) and three 400mm (15.75in) torpedo tubes
POWERPLANT: single shaft, diesel/electric motors
RANGE: not known
PERFORMANCE: surfaced 11 knots; submerged 20 knots

Victor III

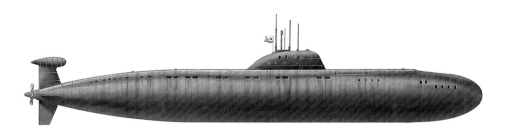

An improvement on the Victor II, the first Victor III class SSN was completed at Komsomolsk in 1978, and production proceeded at a rapid rate at both this yard and Leningrad up to the end of 1984, after which it began to tail off. The Victor III incorporated major advances in acoustic quietening, so that the vessel's radiated noise level is about the same as that of the American Los Angeles class. Apart from anti-ship and ASW submarines and torpedoes, the Victor IIIs are armed with the SS-N-21 Samson submarine-launched cruise missile, which has a range of 3000km (1620nm) at about 0.7M and carries a 200kT nuclear warhead. A total of 25 Victor III class boats was produced, with all but one still operational in the 1990s. Its design successor was the Akula class, the first of which was launched in 1984.

SPECIFICATIONS

COUNTRY: Russia
LAUNCH DATE: 1978
CREW: 100
DISPLACEMENT: surfaced not available; submerged 6400 tonnes (6300 tons)
DIMENSIONS: 104m x 10m x 7m (347ft 9in x 32ft 10in x 23ft)
ARMAMENT: six 533mm (21in) torpedo tubes; SS-N-15/16/21 SSMs
POWERPLANT: single screw, nuclear PWR, turbines
RANGE: unlimited
PERFORMANCE: surfaced 24 knots; submerged 30 knots

Virginia

The Virginia class represents a new direction for US submarines, which had previously been optimised for fighting a major war in deep water. The Virginia class can still carry out this mission, but was designed with an emphasis on shallow-water littoral operations. It is also far cheaper than the Seawolf class. The boat is built as a number of modular structures, which are isolated to reduce the acoustic signature generated by the submarine's systems. Anechoic tiles coating the outer surface of the vessel further reduce noise and sonar return. USS *Virginia* is armed with four 533mm (21in) torpedo tubes capable of launching Harpoon missiles or torpedoes, plus 12 vertical launch containers for Tomahawk missiles. Mines can also be deployed, as can unmanned underwater vehicles. Special forces teams can be delivered using a lock-in/lock-out chamber, and the boat can also host a mini-submarine.

SPECIFICATIONS

COUNTRY: United States
LAUNCH DATE: 16 August 2003
CREW: 134
DISPLACEMENT: submerged 7300 tonnes (7185 tons)
DIMENSIONS: 114.91m x 10.36m (377ft x 34ft)
ARMAMENT: four 533mm torpedo tube; 12 tomahawk in vertical launch containers. Mix of Harpoon missiles and Mk48 torpedoes: total of 40 weapons carried
POWERPLANT: one GE PWR S9G pressurised water nuclear reactor (29,828kW/40,000hp)
RANGE: effectively unlimited
PERFORMANCE: surfaced not known; submerged greater than 25 knots

Volframio

Volframio was one of 13 submarines of the Acciaio class, built in 1941–42 and named after metallic elements or alloys. Nine were lost during World War II, including *Volframio* herself; she was scuttled at La Spezia on 8 September 1943, following the Armistice. She was raised and refloated by the Germans, but was not renamed. She was sunk for the last time by aircraft bombs at La Spezia in 1944. By 1944, most Italian submarines were in very poor condition or completely obsolete, and few were assessed as suitable for refurbishing. The longest surviving vessel of the class was *Giada*, which was removed from the naval list in February 1948 under the terms of the Peace Treaty and converted to a hull for recharging batteries. She reappeared on the naval list in March 1951, and was rebuilt and modified to carry four 533mm (21in) torpedo tubes forward.

SPECIFICATIONS

COUNTRY: Italy
LAUNCH DATE: 09 November 1941
CREW: 46–50
DISPLACEMENT: surfaced 726 tonnes (715 tons); submerged 884 tonnes (870 tons)
DIMENSIONS: 60m x 6.5m x 4.5m (196ft 10in x 21ft 4in x 14ft 9in)
ARMAMENT: four 533mm (21in) torpedo tubes; one 100mm (3.9in) gun
POWERPLANT: two diesels, two electric motors
RANGE: 7042km (3800nm) at 10 knots
PERFORMANCE: surfaced 15 knots; submerged 7.7 knots

Walrus (1959)

HMS *Walrus* was one of the eight-strong Porpoise class; these were the first operational British submarines designed after the war to be accepted into service. They were large boats with a good radius of action, which meant that they were able to undertake continuous submerged patrols in any part of the world. The design stress, in fact, was on endurance, both on the surface and submerged, whether on batteries or 'snorting'. The snorkel equipment was designed to give maximum charging facilities and to operate in rough sea conditions. Both air and surface warning radar could be operated at periscope depth as well as on the surface. The boats in the class were *Cachalot*, *Finwhale*, *Grampus*, *Narwhal*, *Porpoise*, *Rorqual*, *Sealion* and *Walrus*; the latter continued in service until the early 1980s.

SPECIFICATIONS

COUNTRY: United Kingdom
LAUNCH DATE: 22 September 1959
CREW: 71
DISPLACEMENT: surfaced 2062 tonnes (2030 tons); submerged 2444 tonnes (2405 tons)
DIMENSIONS: 73.5m x 8.1m x 5.5m (241ft 2in x 26ft 6in x 18ft 1in)
ARMAMENT: eight 533mm (21in) torpedo tubes
POWERPLANT: two shafts, diesel/electric motors
RANGE: 16,677km (9000nm) at 10 knots
PERFORMANCE: surfaced 12 knots; submerged 17 knots

Walrus (1985)

In 1972, the Royal Netherlands Navy identified a need for a new class of submarine to replace the elderly Dolfijn and Potvis classes. The new design evolved as the Walrus class, and was based on the Zwaardvis hull form with similar dimensions and silhouette, but with more automation, a smaller crew, more modern electronics, X-configuration control surfaces and the French MAREI high-tensile steel hull material that permits a 50 per cent increase in maximum diving depth to 300m (985ft). The first unit, *Walrus*, was laid down in 1979 for commissioning in 1986, but, in August that year, she suffered a serious fire (enough to make her hull glow white-hot) while in the final stage of completion, so she was not completed until 1991. Despite the intensity of the blaze, her hull had luckily escaped serious damage.

SPECIFICATIONS

COUNTRY: Netherlands
LAUNCH DATE: October 1985
CREW: 49
DISPLACEMENT: surfaced 2490 tonnes (2450 tons); submerged 2800 tonnes (2755 tons)
DIMENSIONS: 67.5m x 8.4m x 6.6m (221ft 5in x 27ft 7in x 21ft 8in)
ARMAMENT: four 533mm (21in) torpedo tubes
POWERPLANT: single screw, diesel/electric motors
RANGE: 18,520km (10,000nm) at 9 knots
PERFORMANCE: surfaced 13 knots; submerged 20 knots

Warspite

The bearer of a famous name in British naval history, HMS *Warspite* was the third of the Royal Navy's nuclear attack submarines to be ordered from Vickers-Armstrong; she and her predecessor *Valiant* were slightly larger than *Dreadnought*. Work on both SSNs was held up because of the urgent need to bring the Polaris missile-armed submarines of the Resolution class into service to replace the RAF's V-bombers in the strategic QRA role, and *Warspite* was not completed until April 1967. She was followed by three Churchill-class vessels, which were modified Valiant-class SSNs and were somewhat quieter in service, having benefited from the experience gained in operating the earlier boats. *Valiant* and *Warspite*, together with the Churchills, were paid off in the late 1980s, following the full deployment of the Trafalgar class SSNs.

SPECIFICATIONS

COUNTRY: United Kingdom
LAUNCH DATE: 25 September 1965
CREW: 116
DISPLACEMENT: surfaced 4470 tonnes (4400 tons); submerged 4979 tonnes (4900 tons)
DIMENSIONS: 86.9m x 10.1m x 8.2m (285ft 1in x 33ft 3in x 27ft)
ARMAMENT: six 533mm (21in) torpedo tubes
POWERPLANT: nuclear, one PWR
RANGE: unlimited
PERFORMANCE: surfaced 20 knots; submerged 29 knots

Whiskey

The Soviet Union's first post-war submarine, and essentially a modified version of the German Type XXI design, the Russians mass-produced 236 Whiskey class diesel-electric submarines between 1949 and 1957, using prefabricated sections. All the early variants (*Whiskey* I–IV) were eventually converted to the Whiskey V configuration, with no gun armament and a streamlined sail. Some were configured for special duties operations, fitted with a deck-mounted lockout diving chamber for use by Special Forces' combat swimmers. A submarine of this class (No 137) went aground inside Swedish territorial waters on 27 October 1981, near Karlskrona naval base, providing evidence that the Whiskey boats were routinely engaged in clandestine activities. Some 45 Whiskey boats were transferred to countries friendly to the Soviet Union.

SPECIFICATIONS

COUNTRY: Russia
LAUNCH DATE: 1949 (first unit)
CREW: 50
DISPLACEMENT: surfaced 1066 tonnes (1050 tons); submerged 1371 tonnes (1350 tons)
DIMENSIONS: 76m x 6.5m x 5m (249ft 4in x 21ft 4in x 16ft 5in)
ARMAMENT: four 533mm (21in) and two 406mm (16in) torpedo tubes
POWERPLANT: twin screws, diesel/electric motors
RANGE: 15,890km (8580nm) at 10 knots
PERFORMANCE: surfaced 18 knots; submerged 14 knots

X1 (1955)

An experimental vessel, *X1* was intended to be the prototype of a series of midget submarines capable of penetrating the defences of enemy harbours, and her design was based on that of the British *X5*. *X1* normally carried a four-man crew, but on short missions she could accommodate six. She was originally fitted with a hydrogen-peroxide propulsion unit, which allowed her diesel engines to be used while submerged, and a small electric motor was fitted to allow her to 'creep' silently under water. In 1960, a hydrogen peroxide explosion blew off her bow section; the remainder of the boat remained intact. She was laid up in 1960 after repair, and later used for research purposes until 1973. *X1* was the only midget submarine built for the US Navy, which had never identified a need for such craft.

SPECIFICATIONS

COUNTRY: United States
LAUNCH DATE: 7 September 1955
CREW: 4–6
DISPLACEMENT: surfaced 31 tonnes (30.5 tons); submerged 36 tonnes (35.4 tons)
DIMENSIONS: 15m x 2m x 2m (49ft 3in x 6ft 7in x 6ft 7in)
ARMAMENT: none
POWERPLANT: single screw, diesel/electric motors
RANGE: over 926km (500nm)
PERFORMANCE: surfaced 15 knots; submerged 12 knots

X5

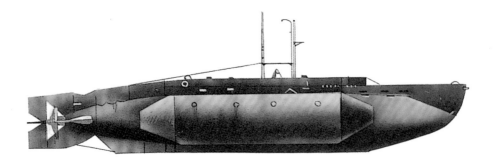

No provision was made before World War II for 'midget' submarines in the Royal Navy, and their design and production was a purely wartime expedient. Two prototypes, *X3* and *X4*, were built, from which an operational X-type (including *X5*) was developed. The most notable event involving the class was the unsuccessful attempt to sink the German battleship *Tirpitz*. A number of X-craft were towed to Altenfjord, in northern Norway, where German surface units lay at anchor. Having successfully negotiated the minefields and barrages protecting the German ships, *X6* and *X7* managed to lay charges that damaged the battleship and put her out of action, but *X5* disappeared without trace during the mission. X-craft were also used successfully against Japanese shipping in Singapore in 1945.

SPECIFICATIONS

COUNTRY: United States
LAUNCH DATE: 1942
CREW: 4
DISPLACEMENT: surfaced 27 tonnes (26.5 tons); submerged 30 tons (29.5 tons)
DIMENSIONS: 15.7m x 1.8m x 2.6m (51ft 6in x 6ft x 8ft 6in)
ARMAMENT: explosive charges
POWERPLANT: single screw, diesel/electric motors
RANGE: not recorded
PERFORMANCE: surfaced 6.5 knots; submerged 5 knots

Xia class

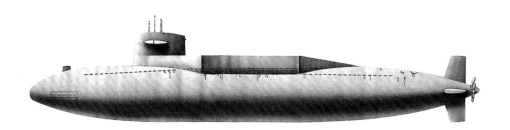

The first type of nuclear ballistic-missile submarine built by the People's Republic of China, *Xia* is roughly similar to the Russian Yankee II missile boat. The first launch of a JL-1 SLBM took place on 30 April 1982, from a submerged position near Hulodao in the Yellow Sea. The second was launched on 12 October 1982 from a specially-modified Golf-class trials submarine, and the first launch from *Xia* herself was made in 1985. It was unsuccessful, delaying the submarine's entry into service while modifications were carried out. A satisfactory launch was finally made on 27 September 1988. The JL-1 missile had a range of 1800km (972nm) and carries a single 350kT warhead. A second Xia class boat was launched in 1982, and there are unconfirmed reports that one of the pair was lost in an accident.

SPECIFICATIONS

COUNTRY: China
LAUNCH DATE: 30 April 1981
CREW: 140
DISPLACEMENT: surfaced not known; submerged 6604 tonnes (6500 tons)
DIMENSIONS: 120m x 10m x 8m (393ft 7in x 32ft 10in x 26ft 2in)
ARMAMENT: six 533mm (21in) torpedo tubes; 12 JL-1 SLBMs
POWERPLANT: single shaft, nuclear PWR, turbo-electric drive
RANGE: unlimited
PERFORMANCE: surfaced not known; submerged 22 knots

Yankee class

During the Cold War period, three or four Yankee boats were on station at any one time off the eastern seaboard of the US, with a further unit either on transit to or from a patrol area. The forward-deployed Yankees were assigned the wartime role of destroying targets such as SAC bomber alert bases and carriers/SSBNs in port, and of disrupting the American higher command echelons to ease the task of follow up ICBM strikes. As they progressively retired from their SSBN role, some Yankees were converted to carry cruise or anti-ship missiles as SSNs. Despite the removal of the ballistic missile section the overall length of the Yankee's hull has increased by 12m (39.4ft) with the insertion of a 'notch waisted' central section, housing three tubes amidships on either side, and the magazine holds up to 35 SS-N-21s or additional torpedoes and mines.

SPECIFICATIONS

COUNTRY: Russia
LAUNCH DATE: 1967
CREW: 120
DISPLACEMENT: surfaced 7925 tonnes (7800 tons); submerged 9450 tonnes (9300 tons)
DIMENSIONS: 129.5m x 11.6m x 7.8m (424ft 10in x 38ft 1in x 25ft 7in)
ARMAMENT: six 533mm (21in) torpedo tubes; 16 SS-N-6 missiles
POWERPLANT: twin screws, two nuclear PWRs, turbines
RANGE: unlimited
PERFORMANCE: surfaced 20 knots; submerged 30 knots

Zeeleeuw

The *Zeeleeuw* (Sealion) is a Walrus-class SSK, a design based on the Zwaardvis hull form with similar dimensions and silhouette, but with more automation, a smaller crew, more modern electronics, X-configuration control surfaces and the French MAREI high-tensile steel hull material that permits a 50 per cent increase in maximum diving depth to 300m (985ft). The first unit, *Walrus*, was laid down in 1979 for commissioning in 1986, but in August that year she suffered a serious fire that destroyed her wiring and computers while in the final stage of completion, so she was not commissioned until March 1992, two years after *Zeeleeuw*. The other two vessels in the class are *Dolfijn* and *Bruinvis*. Two submarines of this class are in service with the Taiwanese Navy; they were the first to be exported by the Netherlands.

SPECIFICATIONS

COUNTRY: Netherlands
LAUNCH DATE: 20 June 1987
CREW: 49
DISPLACEMENT: surfaced 2490 tonnes (2450 tons); submerged 2800 tonnes (2755 tons)
DIMENSIONS: 67.5m x 8.4m x 6.6m (221ft 5in x 27ft 7in x 21ft 8in)
ARMAMENT: four 533mm (21in) torpedo tubes
POWERPLANT: single screw, diesel/electric motors
RANGE: 18,520km (10,000nm) at 9 knots
PERFORMANCE: surfaced 13 knots; submerged 20 knots

Index

A

Acciaio 24
Agosta 25
Alaska (Ohio Class) 26
Albacore 27
Alfa 28
Aluminaut 29
Arihant 30
Astute (S119) 31

B

BGM-109 Tomahawk 32
Barracuda Class 33
Borei Class 34

C

Casma (Type 209) 35
CB12 36
Charlie I Class 37
Charlie II Class 38
Collins 39
Conqueror 40

D

Daniel Boone 41
Daphné 42
DCTN F17 43
Deep Quest 44
Deepstar 4000 45
Delta I 46
Delta III 47
Diablo 48
Dolfijn 49
Doris 50
Dreadbought 51
Drum 52
DTCN L5 53

E

Enrico Tazzoli 54
Enrico Toti 55
Entemedor 56
Evangelista Torricelli 57
Explorer 58

F

FFV Tp42 series 59
FFV Tp61 series 60
Flutto 61
Foxtrot class 62

G

Gal 63
Galerna 64
George Washington 65
George Washington Carver 66
Giuliano Prini 67
Golf I 68
Grayback 69
Grongo 70
Grouper 71

H

Ha 201 Class 72
Hai Lung 73
Han 74
Harpoon 75

Harushio (1967)
Harushio (1989)

I

I 201 78
I 351 79
I 400 80
India 81

K

Kilo Class 82

L

Le Terrible 83
Le Triomphant 84
Los Angeles 85

M

M4 86
Marlin 87
Marsopa 88
Mk 37 89
Mk 46 90
Mk 48 91

N

Näcken 92
Narwhal 93
Nautilus 94
Nazario Sauro 95
November Class 96

O

Oberon 97
Oscar Class 98
Oyashio 99

P

Papa 100
Pickerel 101
Piper 102
Polaris A3 103
Poseidon C3 104

R

Redoutable 105
Remo 106
Requin 107
Resolution 108
RO-100 109
Roland Morillot 110
Romeo 111
Rubis 112

S

San Francisco 113
Sanguine 114
Santa Cruz 115
Scorpène 116
Seawolf Class 117
Sentinel 118
Seraph 119
Severodvinsk (Graney Class) 120
Shark 121
Sierra Class 122
Siroco 123
Sjöormen 124
Skate 125

Skipjack 126
Soryu Class 127
Spearfish 128
SS-N-18 129
SS-N-20 130
SS-N-6 131
Sting Ray 132
Storm 133
Strugeon 134
Sub-Martel 135
Swiftsure 136

T

Tang 137
Tango 138
Thomson-Sintra 139
Thresher/Permit Class 140
Tigerfish 141
Torbay 142
Trafalgar 143
Triton 144
Type 039 Song Class 145
Type 093 146
Type 214 (classe Papanikolis U214) 147
Type 640 148
Typhoon 149

U

U12 150
U1081 152
U2326 153
U2501 154
U2511 155
U28 151
UGM-96A Trident I C4 156
Upholder 157

V

V Class 158
Valiant 159
Vanguard 160
Västergötland 161
Victor III 162
Virginia 163
Volframio 164

W

Walrus (1959) 165
Walrus (1985) 166
Warspite 167
Whiskey 168

X

X1 1955 169
X5 170
Xia Class 171

Y

Yankee Class 172

Z

Zeeleeuw 173